D1270288

The 12 Questions That Keep Family Business Directors Awake at Night

Travis W. Harms, CFA, CPA/ABV

The 12 Questions That Keep Family Business Directors Awake at Night

ISBN: 978-0-9825364-6-9

Mercer Capital
5100 Poplar Avenue
Suite 2600
Memphis, Tennessee 38137
901.685.2120

Table of Contents

Introduction

Mercer Capital provides sophisticated corporate finance services to family businesses throughout the nation. We know that stewarding a multi-generation family business is a privilege that comes with certain responsibilities, and each family business faces a unique set of challenges at any given time. For some, shareholder engagement is not currently an issue, but establishing a workable management accountability program is. For others, dividend policy is easy, while next gen development weighs heavily. Through our family business advisory services practice, we work with successful families facing issues like these every day.

Our goal for this book is to address the most common questions and challenges facing family business directors. Since we have striven for brevity—not to mention the fact that we don't pretend to have all the answers—the chapters have been constructed to help you think through these questions. At the end of each chapter, we offer a list of potential action items to help family business leaders and directors prioritize which issues are most pressing to the long-term health and sustainability of the business.

- **How Do We Promote Positive Shareholder Engagement?** As families grow into the fourth and fifth generations, common ownership of a successful business can serve as the glue that holds the family together. However, as the proportion of non-employee family shareholders increases, maintaining productive shareholder engagement grows more challenging.

- **How Do We Communicate More Effectively with Shareholders?** Effective communication is a critical for any relationship. Multi-generation family businesses are complex relationship webs. Identifying best practices for communicating effectively with family shareholders is a common objective for family businesses.

- **Does Our Dividend Policy Fit?** Hands down, the most frequent topic of conversation with clients is establishing a dividend policy that balances the lifestyle needs and aspirations of family shareholders with the needs of the business.

- **To Invest or Not to Invest?** The flip-side of dividend policy is how to invest for growth. Can the family business keep up with the biological growth of the family? Is that a desirable goal? Regardless of the target, family business leaders are concerned about identifying and executing investments to support the growth of the family business.

- **Should We Diversify?** We find that a striking number of the family businesses diversify rather far afield from the legacy business of the founding generation. What are the marks of effective diversification for a family business?

- **Does Father Always Know Best?** Evaluating managerial performance is never easy; adding kinship ties to the mix only makes things dicier. The family business leaders we speak with are eager to develop and implement effective management accountability structures.

- **How Do We Find Our Next Leader?** Whether it comes simply through age or as a result of poor performance, management succession is somewhere on the horizon for every family business.

- **Is There a Ticking Time Bomb Lurking in Our Family Business?** Buy-sell agreements don't matter until they do. When written well and understood by all the parties, buy-sell agreements can minimize headaches when a family business hits one of life's inevitable potholes. But far too many are written poorly and/or misunderstood. Directors are always eager to discuss best practices for buy-sell agreements.

- **What Is the Family's Most Valuable Asset?** Rising generations are naturally more diffuse than prior generations with regard to geography, interests, skill sets, and desires. Family leaders are interested in identifying appropriate pathways for the next generation to engage, learn, and grow in their contribution to, and impact upon, the family business.

- **What Should We Do About Estate Taxes?** Directors are keenly interested in tax-efficient techniques for transferring ownership of the family business to succeeding generations. While certainly important, there may be unanticipated pitfalls if estate and other taxes are the only factors considered when transferring wealth.

- **How Should We Respond to an Acquisition Offer?** Even if the family does not plan to sell, credible acquisition offers at what appear to be attractive financial terms need to be assessed. It is important to know how best to evaluate and respond to such offers.

- **Who's In and Who's Out?** There are many reasons family members may want to sell shares: desire for diversification, major life changes, funding for estate tax payments, starting a new business, or funding other major expenditures. What is the best way to provide liquidity to family shareholders on fair terms without sparking a run on the bank?

Continuing the Conversation

Our weekly blog, *Family Business Director*, addresses the issues and challenges covered in this book. For a more in-depth conversation including examples and case studies, visit the blog at mer.cr/fbdirector.

The 12 Questions

CHAPTER ONE

How Do We Promote Positive Shareholder Engagement?

Does it matter whether family shareholders are engaged with the business? What does positive engagement even look like? Does the investment of time and effort required to develop positive shareholder engagement actually provide a return to the family? These and similar questions weigh heavily on the minds of many multi-generational family business leaders.

Why Is Shareholder Engagement Important for Family Businesses?

As family businesses mature into the third and subsequent generations, it becomes less and less likely that extended family members will be both share-holders and active participants in the business. As families grow numerically, they tend to become more geographically dispersed. Lack of professional involvement in the business, combined with geographic separation, can result in family shareholders feeling disconnected and becoming disengaged from the family business. A successful multi-generation family business can promote healthy family cohesion, but when shareholders are not positively engaged, the business can quickly turn into a source of stress and family strife.

Some families choose to eliminate the existence of disengaged shareholders by limiting share ownership to those members that are actively involved in the business. While this may be an appropriate solution for some families, it can have the unintended consequence of creating distinct classes of economic haves and have-nots within the family. When that occurs, the business quickly ceases to be a center of family unity.

For most businesses, there simply is no necessary link between share ownership and active involvement in the company. If public companies can function well with non-employee owners, surely it is possible for family businesses to do so as well. But to do so, family businesses will need to be diligent to promote positive shareholder engagement.

The Marks of an Engaged Shareholder

It might be tempting to label non-employee shareholders as "passive," but we suspect that term does not do justice to the ideal relationship between the company and such shareholders. "Actively non-controlling" hits closer to the mark but doesn't exactly trip off the tongue. If "passive" is not the ideal, the following characteristics can be used to identify positively engaged shareholders.

- **An appreciation of what the business means to the family.** Engaged shareholders know the history of the family business in its broad outline. Few things promote a sense of community like a shared story. A successful family business provides a narrative legacy that few families possess. Engaged shareholders embrace, extend, and re-tell the story of the family business.

- **A willingness to participate.** Full-time employment is not the only avenue for participating in the family business. Engaged shareholders understand their responsibility to be active participants in the groups that are appropriate to their skills, life stage, and interests, which may include serving as a director, sitting on an owners' council, or participating in a family council.

- **A willingness to listen.** Positively-engaged non-employee shareholders recognize that there are issues affecting the family business, the industry, and the company's customers and suppliers of which they are unaware. As a result, they are willing to listen to management, regardless of whether management consists primarily of non-family professionals or the shareholder's second cousins.

- **A willingness to develop informed opinions.** A willingness to listen does not mean passive acceptance of everything management is communicating. A competent and confident management team recognizes that non-employee shareholders have expertise, experiences, and insights that members of management lack. Engaged shareholders acknowledge their responsibility to develop and share informed opinions, not just gut reactions or prejudices.

- **A willingness to consider perspectives of other shareholder groups.** Engaged shareholders do not seek the benefit of their own branch of the family tree to the detriment of the others. Multi-generation family businesses inevitably have distinct shareholder "clienteles" with unique sets of risk tolerances and return preferences. Privileging the perspective of a single shareholder clientele is a sure way to promote discord.

> Most of the intra-family shareholder disputes we have seen are ultimately traceable to shareholders that over time became disengaged from the business.

- **A commitment to deal fairly.** Fairness needs to run in both directions: non-employee shareholders should not be penalized for not working in the business, and shareholders that do work in the business need to be fully and fairly compensated for their efforts. Fairness also extends to distribution and redemption policy, both of which can be used to the disadvantage of one group within the family. Engaged shareholders are committed to fair dealing in transactions with the business and within the family.

How to Develop an Engaged Shareholder Base

The "how" of shareholder engagement is closely related to the characteristics of engaged shareholders noted above.

- **Develop mechanisms for appropriate involvement.** Not everyone can have a seat at the board, but family and owner's councils can be great ways to broaden opportunities and prepare family members for greater involvement.

- **Emphasize the privilege/responsibility of being a shareholder.** This will look different for every family, but a visible commitment to charitable contributions and service opportunities can be a powerful signal to the family that being a shareholder involves a stewardship that transcends simply receiving dividends.

- **Basic financial education.** Family members will have many different talents, interests, and competencies. Offering rudimentary financial education (i.e., how to read a financial statement, and understanding how distribution policy influences reinvestment) can empower the healthcare professionals, educators, and engineers in the family to develop and communicate informed opinions on family business matters.

- **Actively solicit shareholder feedback.** While it is true that the squeaky wheel gets the grease, it is often the un-squeaky wheels that have the most valuable insight. Periodic shareholder surveys can be an effective tool for promoting positive shareholder engagement.

- **Demonstrate a commitment to fair dealing.** Shareholders who are also managers in the business need to be wary of the tendency to pursue empire-building activities at the expense of providing appropriate returns on the shares in the family business.

Most of the intra-family shareholder disputes we have seen (and we have witnessed too many) are ultimately traceable to shareholders that over time became disengaged from the business. Family business directors who focus on positive shareholder engagement today can prevent a lot of grief tomorrow.

Potential Next Steps

- ☐ Create / document / update the history of the family business

- ☐ Identify the two or three turning points in the history of the business that define the family's values and commitments

- ☐ Evaluate current membership of governing/advisory bodies (i.e., board of directors, owners' council, or family council)

- ☐ Provide basic financial education opportunities for family shareholders

- ☐ Conduct a shareholder survey to identify the concerns, preferences, and risk tolerances of the family shareholders

CHAPTER TWO

How Do We Communicate More Effectively with Shareholders?

Communication determines the success of any relationship, and the relationships among shareholders of multi-generation family businesses are no exception. In the early years of a family business, communication is generally informal (and continual), since the dining room often doubles as the board room. As the business and family grow, the shareholder relationships become more complicated, and formal communication becomes more important.

For a multi-generation family business, communication is not optional. A failure to communicate is a communication failure. When communication is lacking, the default assumption of shareholders—especially those not actively involved in the business—will be that management and the directors are hiding something. Suspicion breeds discontent; prolonged discontent solidifies into rancor and, in some cases, litigation.

In light of the dire consequences of poor communication, how can family business directors develop effective and sustainable communication programs? We suggest that public companies can provide a great template for multi-generation family businesses. It is perhaps ironic that public companies—to whom their shareholder bases are largely anonymous—are typically more diligent in their shareholder communications than family businesses, whose shareholders are literally next of kin. While public companies' shareholder communications are legally mandated, forward-thinking public companies view the required shareholder communications not as regulatory requirements to be met, but as opportunities to tell their story in a compelling way.

There are probably only a handful of family businesses for which shareholder communication needs to be as frequent and detailed as that required by the SEC. The structure and discipline of SEC reporting is what needs to be emulated. For family businesses, the goal is to communicate, not inundate. At some point, too much information can simply turn into noise. Family business managers and directors should tailor a shareholder communication program along the following dimensions:

- **Frequency.** Public companies communicate results quarterly. Depending on the nature of the business and the desires of the shareholder base, less frequent communication may be appropriate for a family business. The frequency of communication should correspond to the natural intervals over which (1) genuinely "new" information about the company's results, competitive environment, and strategy is available, and (2) shareholders perceive that the most recent communication has become "stale." As a result, there is no one-size-fits-all frequency; what is most important is the discipline of a schedule.

- **Level of detail.** Public company reports are quite detailed. Family business leaders should assess what level of detail is appropriate for shareholder communications. If the goal is to communicate, the appropriate level of detail should be defined with reference to that which is necessary to tell the company's story. The detail needs to be presented to shareholders with sufficient supporting context regarding the company's historical performance and conditions in the relevant industries and economy. A dashboard approach that focuses on key metrics, as illustrated in Figure 1, can be an effective tool for focusing attention on the measures that matter.

- **Format/Access.** The advent of accessible webcast and data room technology makes it much easier for family businesses to distribute sensitive financial information securely. Use of such platforms also provides valuable feedback regarding what is working and what is not (since use of the platform by shareholders can be monitored). Some families may have existing newsletters that provide a natural and existing touchpoint for communicating financial results.

- **Emphasis.** The goal of shareholder communication should be to help promote positive shareholder engagement. To that end, the emphasis of the communication should not be simply the bare reporting of historical results, but should emphasize what the results mean for the business in terms of strategy and outlook for the future. It is probably not possible to re-tell the company's story too many times. Shareholders that are not actively involved in the business will be able to internalize the company's strategy only after repeated exposure. What may seem like the annoying repetitions of a broken record to management and directors will for shareholders be the re-exposure necessary to "own" the company's story.

Shareholder communication is an investment, but one that in our experience has an attractive return. To get the most out of the invest-ment, family business leaders must provide the necessary training and education to shareholders so that they will be able confidently to assess and interpret the information communicated. With that foundation in place, a structured communication program can go a long way to ensuring that family shareholders are positively engaged with the business.

> A dashboard approach that focuses on key metrics, as illustrated in Figure 1, can be an effective tool for focusing attention on the measures that matter.

Potential Next Steps

- ☐ Create a schedule of "earnings releases" to the family for the coming year

- ☐ Develop a performance dashboard of relevant metrics for family distribution

- ☐ Identify the best channel for communicating with family shareholders

Figure 1

FOURTH QUARTER 2017

Performance Dashboard

Miller Family Enterprise—Quarterly Performance Dashboard
(Shareholders Only—Not for Distribution)

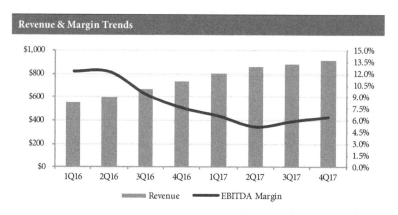

Revenue & Margin Trends

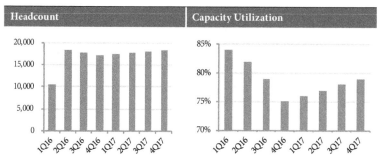

Headcount

Capacity Utilization

Our integration of the SmithCo acquisition in 2Q16 remains ongoing, with capacity utilization continuing to recover toward pre-acquisition levels. Modest increases in headcount contributed to growing revenue. EBITDA margins solidified on improving utilization.

Operating cash flow is sufficient to fund necessary capital expenditures. As we are comfortable with existing debt levels, we expect to continue our recently instituted share repurchase program on a limited basis, complemented by continuing regular dividends.

Figure 1 (continued)

Sources and Use of Cash - LTM			
Sources of Cash		**Uses of Cash**	
Operating Cash Flow	41.1	Capital Expenditures	14.7
Asset Sales	0.3	Business Acquisitions	0.6
Proceeds - Debt	0.0	Debt Repayment	86.2
Proceeds - Equity	115.4	Share Repurchase	26.5
Liquidity Reserves	0.0	Dividends Paid	1.0
		Liquidity Reserves	27.7
TOTAL	**$156.8**	**TOTAL**	**$156.8**

Balance Sheet Summary			
	Dec-17	**Dec-16**	**$ Change**
Cash & equivalents	238.9	201.4	37.5
Other current assets	267.8	230.7	37.0
Total current assets	506.7	432.2	74.5
Net fixed assets	119.0	113.9	5.2
Goodwill & intangibles	265.3	260.5	4.8
Other assets	53.3	59.8	(6.5)
TOTAL ASSETS	**$944.4**	**$866.4**	**$78.0**
Short-term debt	0.0	8.9	(8.9)
Other current liabilities	125.6	105.3	20.3
Total current liabilities	125.6	114.1	11.5
Long-term debt	105.2	181.2	(76.0)
Other liabilities	33.3	26.0	7.3
TOTAL LIABILITIES	**$264.0**	**$321.3**	**($57.3)**
TOTAL EQUITY	**$680.3**	**$545.1**	**$135.2**

CHAPTER THREE

Does Our Dividend Policy Fit?

Our multi-generation family business clients ask us about dividend policy more often than any other topic. This isn't surprising, since returns to family business shareholders come in only two forms: current income from dividends and capital appreciation. For many shareholders, capital appreciation is what makes them wealthy, but current income is what makes them *feel* wealthy.

In other words, dividends are the most transparent expression of what the family business means to the family economically. Knowing what the business "means" to the family is essential for promoting positive shareholder engagement, family harmony, and sustainability. The business may "mean" different things to the family at different times (or, to different members of the family at the same time). In our experience, there are four broad "meanings" that a family business can have. These "meanings" are not mutually exclusive, but one will usually predominate at a given time. Importantly, the "meaning" of the business has implications for dividend policy.

- **Meaning #1 - The family business is an economic growth engine for future generations.** For some families, the business is perceived as a vehicle for increasing per capita family wealth over time. For these families, dividends are likely to take a backseat to reinvestment in the business needed to fuel the growth required to keep pace with the biological growth of the family.

- **Meaning #2 - The family business is a store of value for the family.** For other families, the business is perceived as a means of capital preservation. Amid the volatility of public equity markets, the family business serves as ballast for the family's overall wealth. Dividends are generally modest for these families, with earnings retained, in part, to mitigate potential swings in value.

> In contrast to public companies or those owned by private equity funds, "meaning" will generally trump dispassionate analysis of available investment opportunities.

- **Meaning #3 - The family business is a source of wealth accumulation.** Alternatively, the family business may be perceived as a mechanism for accumulating family wealth outside the business. In these cases, individual family members are expected to use dividends from the business to accumulate wealth through investments in marketable securities, real estate, or other operating businesses. Dividends are emphasized for these families, along with the (potentially unspoken) expectation that distributions will be used by the recipients to diversify away from, and limit dependence on, the family business.

- **Meaning #4 - The family business is a source of lifestyle.** Finally, the business may be perceived as maintaining the family's lifestyle. Dividends are not necessarily expected to fund a life of idle leisure, but are relied upon by family shareholders to supplement income from careers and other sources for home and auto purchases, education expenses, weddings, travel, philanthropy, etc. These businesses typically have moderate reinvestment needs, and predictability of the dividend stream is often more important to shareholders than real (i.e., net of inflation) growth in the dividend. Continuation of the dividend is the primary measure the family uses to evaluate management's performance.

From a textbook perspective, dividends are treated as a residual: once attractive reinvestment opportunities have been exhausted, the remaining

Figure 2

Family Business "Meaning"	Implications for Dividend Policy
Growth Engine for Future Generations	**Dividends:** None or token amount **Optimal Characteristics:** Businesses with abundant attractive reinvestment opportunities **Risks:** Business may make riskier investments in order to achieve target returns amid heavy reinvestment
Store of Value	**Dividends:** Higher payouts possible, but distributions often perceived as detrimental to the safety of the business **Optimal Characteristics:** Maturing businesses in stable, or counter-cyclical industries **Risks:** May accumulate low-yielding, non-operating assets which create a drag on shareholder returns
Source of Wealth Accumulation	**Dividends:** Expected to be high so that individual shareholders can diversify and reduce economic dependence on the family business **Optimal Characteristics:** Mature businesses with limited attractive reinvestment opportunities **Risks:** May lose existing competitive advantages if profitable reinvestment opportunities are foregone in favor of distributions
Source of Lifestyle	**Dividends:** Expected to be stable and (ideally) growing from a sustainable base regardless of annual business fluctuations **Optimal Characteristics:** Growing businesses with moderate reinvestment needs to fund organic growth opportunities **Risks:** Emphasis on predictability of dividends may lead to excess asset accumulation and/or limited reinvestment at inopportune times

cash flow should be distributed to the shareholders. However, at a practical level, the different potential "meanings" assigned to the business by the family will, to some degree, circumscribe the dividend policy alternatives available to the directors. For example, eliminating dividends in favor of increased reinvestment is not a practical alternative for family businesses in the third or fourth categories above, regardless of how abundant attractive investment opportunities may be.

Figure 2 on the prior page illustrates the relationship between "meaning" and dividend policy.

The textbook perspective on dividend policy is valid, but can be adhered to only within the context of the "meaning" assigned to the family business. In contrast to public companies or those owned by private equity funds, "meaning" will generally trump dispassionate analysis of available investment opportunities. If family business leaders conclude that the "meaning" assigned to the business by the family does not align with the optimal dividend policy, the priority should

Figure 3

Policy	Description
Fixed Payment	The board declares a fixed annual dollar dividend, and the Company can reinvest the residual
Fixed Payout	The board sets the dividend relative to earnings during the period
Fixed Yield	The board sets the dividend relative to the value of the Company
Residual	The board assesses how much can be reinvested in financially attractive projects and sets the dividend equal to the residual

Greater Shareholder Certainty (upward arrow, left)

Greater Board Discretion (downward arrow, right)

be given to changing what the business "means" to the family. Once the change in "meaning" has been embraced by the family, the change in dividend policy will more naturally follow.

A dividend policy describes how the family business determines distributions on a year-to-year basis. A consistent dividend policy helps family shareholders understand, predict, and evaluate dividend decisions made by the board of directors. Potential family business dividend policies can be arrayed on a spectrum that ranges from maximum shareholder certainty to maximum board discretion.

Family shareholders should know what the company's current dividend policy is. As evident from Figure 3, knowing the dividend policy does not necessarily mean that one will know the dollar dividend for that year. However, a consistently-communicated and understandable dividend policy contributes greatly to developing positive shareholder engagement.

So what should your family business's dividend policy be? Answering that question requires looking inward and outward. Looking inward, what does the business "mean" to the family? Looking outward, are attractive investment opportunities abundant or scarce? Once the inward and outward perspectives are properly aligned, the dividend policy that is appropriate to the company can be determined by the board and communicated to shareholders.

Potential Next Steps

- Calculate historical shareholder returns, distinguishing returns attributable to capital appreciation from those attributable to distributions

- Assess what the business "means" to the family economically

- Evaluate how the prevailing "meaning" of the business corresponds to the challenges and opportunities facing the business

- Identify the target capital structure for the family business

- Articulate a predictable dividend policy and communicate that policy to family shareholders

CHAPTER FOUR

To Invest or Not to Invest?

Successful family businesses are built over time, and building well requires investment. Since a given dollar of cash flow generated by a business will either be returned to capital providers or reinvested in the business, a company's reinvestment policy is essentially the inverse of its dividend policy: businesses that reinvest heavily will make modest distributions, while those that emphasize large distributions will have less available for reinvestment in the business.

Cash used for dividends leaves the business, providing current returns to investors, while reinvested funds remain in the business with the expectation that the retained capital will generate returns which contribute to capital appreciation. In other words, the tradeoff between current return and capital appreciation is rooted in the corresponding tradeoff between dividends and reinvestment.

For a family business, investment can take different forms.

- **Capacity maintenance and modernization.** Tangible assets wear out, and technological advances can render existing assets inefficient relative to available replacement assets. It may be possible to defer certain expenditures with few observable consequences in the short-term, but the bill always comes due eventually. While investments in capacity maintenance and modernization are not always the most exciting, successful family businesses recognize their priority for long-term sustainability.

- **Capacity Expansion.** In our experience, businesses are either growing or dying—holding steady is nearly impossible over the long-term.

Figure 4

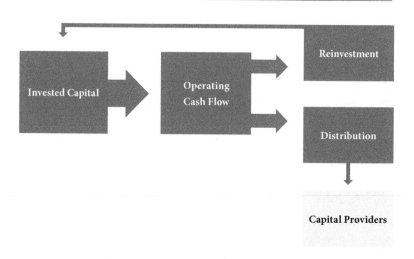

Investments in capacity expansion help keep family businesses on a growth footing. Depending on the company's circumstances, growth investments may involve penetrating new geographic markets, introducing new product lines, or research to develop products for an unmet market need.

- **Acquisitions.** Rather than building incremental capacity, managers and directors of a family business may determine that it is more efficient to assimilate existing industry capacity through an acquisition. Acquisitions offer the opportunity to "hit the ground running" with a built-in customer base, workforce, tradename and other intangible assets that typically accrue slowly over time. On the other hand, acquisitions present integration and culture challenges (and the risk of over-payment) not relevant to other forms of investment. For perspective, during the most recent year, the companies in the S&P 600 small cap index spent $24.2 billion on acquisitions, compared to $28.7 billion on capital expenditures, with nearly 40% of the companies having completed at least one acquisition.

- **Diversification.** Acquisitions are often classified as either vertical (purchase of a supplier or customer) or horizontal (purchase of a competitor). Both types of acquisitions have some organic connection to the existing business.

Sometimes, however, family businesses make investments that are unrelated to legacy operations. It is not uncommon for family businesses to make investments for the sake of diversification, particularly as the business matures and the number of shareholding generations increases.

One of my favorite *Seinfeld* moments (among many) is set at the car rental counter, where an exasperated Jerry explains to the uncomprehending agent the difference between *taking* a reservation and *holding* a reservation. Taking

> Making growth investments is easy, making *good* growth investments is hard.

the reservation is easy, but holding the reservation is what really matters. In the same way, investing for growth is easy: there are plenty of equipment dealers eager to sell shiny new machines and investment bankers who can't wait to describe an exciting acquisition target. But making *good* investments—those for which the tradeoff between current returns and capital appreciation is worthwhile—is considerably harder. So, what are the marks of a good investment?

- **Market opportunity.** A good investment addresses an identifiable need in the market. Further, given the competitive environment in the relevant markets, the identified need can be met profitably. In other words, management should have a simple and straightforward answer to the threshold question: *Why does this investment make sense?*

- **Strategic fit.** Family business managers and directors should also have a concise and credible answer to the natural follow-up question: *Why does this investment make sense for us?* In other words, how does the proposed investment complement the company's corporate strategy? If it extends or deviates from the current strategy, why is the strategy adjustment appropriate? As we described in the context of dividend policy, the business can have a variety of potential "meanings" to the family—does the proposed investment cohere with the "meaning" of the family business?

- **Financially vetted.** A thorough capital budgeting process will involve calculating relevant return measures (internal rate of return, net present value) to assess whether the investment opportunity is likely to increase or decrease the value of the family business. Of course, figures lie and liars make spreadsheets. For a proposed investment that addresses a real market opportunity and is a strategic fit for the company, the financial vetting process should be geared to answering another vital question: *What financial results are necessary for this investment to be good for us?* Has management assembled a compelling case for the expected returns, or is the investment more of a "trust me" exercise?

- **Plan for monitoring.** The most often neglected component of the capital budgeting process is establishing a feedback mechanism for the investment. Too often, capital investments simply melt away into the general corporate asset pool, with no reliable means of evaluating whether the investment generated an appropriate return. In other words, *how will we know if this investment was, in fact, good for us?* The ability to evaluate past investments is critical to making better investments in the future.

All family businesses need to evaluate how they are investing for future growth. Managers and directors must navigate carefully between the risks of depressed future returns through over-investment (i.e. empire building) and losing existing competitive advantages through insufficient reinvestment. The long-term sustainability of the family business depends on it.

Potential Next Steps

- ☐ Create a "map" of historical operating cash flows, tracing what portion has been reinvested in the business and what portion has been distributed to capital providers

- ☐ Calculate the current cost of capital for the family business

- ☐ Identify what prospective investments are currently available to the business, classifying them as follows: (1) capacity maintenance and modernization, (2) capacity expansion, (3) acquisitions, and (4) diversification opportunities

- ☐ Evaluate available investment opportunities by assessing the market opportunity, strategic fit, financial feasibility, and ability to monitor

CHAPTER FIVE

Should We Diversify?

Consider the following perspectives on diversification and risk:

> *"Diversification is an established tenet of conservative investment."*
> – Legendary value investor Benjamin Graham

> *"Diversification may preserve wealth, but concentration builds wealth."*
> – Legendary value investor Warren Buffett

The appropriate role of diversification in multi-generation family businesses is not always obvious. One of the most surprising attributes of many successful multi-generation family businesses is just how little the current business activities resemble those of 20, 30, or 40 years ago. In some cases, this is the product of natural evolution in the company's target market or responses to changes in customer demand; in other cases, however, the changes represent deliberate attempts to diversify away from the legacy business.

What is Diversification?

Diversification is simply investing in multiple assets as a means of reducing risk. If one asset in the portfolio takes a big hit, it is likely that some other segment of the portfolio will perform well at the same time, thereby blunting the negative impact on the overall portfolio. The essence of diversification is (lack of) correlation, or co-movement in returns. Investing in multiple assets yields diversification benefits only if the assets behave differently. If the correlation between the assets is high, the diversification benefits will be negligible, while adding assets with low correlations results in a greater level of risk reduction.

To illustrate, consider a family business deciding which of the following three investments to make as shown in Figure 5.

Figure 5

Potential Investment	Expected Return	Correlation to Business
#1 - Capacity Expansion	12%	High
#2 - Purchase of Supplier	10%	Moderate
#3 - Acquisition of Warehouse	9%	Low

There is no unambiguously correct choice for which investment to make. While the capacity expansion project offers the highest expected return, the close correlation of the returns to the existing business indicates that the project will not reduce the risk—or variability of returns—of the company. At the other extreme, the warehouse acquisition has the lowest expected return, but because the returns on the warehouse are essentially uncorrelated to the existing business, the warehouse acquisition reduces the overall risk profile of the business. The correct choice in this case should be made with respect to the risk tolerances of the shareholders and how the investments fit the strategy of the business.

Diversification to Whom?

Business education is no less susceptible to the lure of fads and groupthink than any roving pack of middle schoolers. When I was being indoctrinated in the mid-90s, the catchphrase of the moment was "core competency." If you stared at any organization long enough—or so the theory seemed to go—you were likely to find that it truly excelled at only a few things. Success was assured by focusing exclusively on these "core competencies" and outsourcing anything and everything else to someone who had a—you guessed it—"core competency" in those activities. Conglomerates were out and spin-offs were in. With every organization executing on only their core competencies, world peace and harmony would ensue. Or something like that.

I don't know what the status of "core competency" is in business schools today, but it does raise an interesting question for family businesses: whose perspective is most important in thinking about diversification? If the relevant perspective is that of the family business itself, the investment and distribution decisions will be made with a view to managing the abso-

> There are no right or wrong answers when it comes to risk tolerance, but there are tradeoffs that need to be acknowledged and communicated plainly.

lute risk of the family business. If instead the relevant perspective is that of the shareholders, investment and distribution decisions are properly made with a view to how the family business contributes to the risk of the shareholders' total wealth (family business plus other assets).

Figure 6

Perspective of the Family Business Shareholder
Make investment and distribution decisions with regard to the contribution of the family business to the risk of the shareholders' total wealth

Perspective of the Family Business	
Make investment and distribution decisions with regard to the risk of the family business itself	**Other Portfolio Investments**

Modern finance theory suggests that for public companies, the shareholder perspective should be what is relevant. Shareholders construct portfolios, and presumably the core competency of risk management resides with them. Corporate managers should therefore not attempt to diversify, because shareholders can do so more efficiently and inexpensively. In other words, corporate managers should stick to their core competencies and not worry about diversification.

That's all well and good for public companies, but for family businesses, the most critical underlying assumptions—ready liquidity and absolute shareholder freedom in constructing one's portfolio—simply do not hold. Family business shares are illiquid and often constitute a large proportion of the shareholders' total wealth. Further, as families mature, shareholder perspectives will inevitably diverge.

Figure 7

Family Business "Meaning"	Implications for Diversification
Growth Engine for Future Generations	Consistent with the Buffett quote above, managers may favor concentrated (undiversified) operations and holdings as a means of maximizing capital appreciation.
Store of Value	Consistent with the Graham quote above, managers are likely to emphasize diversification as a means of minimizing undesirable volatility in reported operating results and value.
Source of Wealth Accumulation	Emphasis on diversification at the shareholder level. Substantial dividends paid as a tool to facilitate shareholder diversification.
Source of Lifestyle	Depending on available reinvestment opportunities, managers may pursue a diversification strategy in bid to minimize risk of disruption to established dividend.

For example, consider two cousins: Sam has devoted his career to managing a non-profit clinic for the underprivileged, and Dave has enjoyed an illustrious career with a white-shoe law firm. Both are 50 years old and both own 5% of the family business. Sam's 5% ownership interest accounts for a significantly larger proportion of his total wealth than does Dave's corresponding 5% ownership interest. As a result, they are likely to have very different perspectives on the role and value of diversification for the family business. Sam will be much more concerned with the absolute risk of the business, whereas Dave will be more interested in how the business contributes to the risk of his overall portfolio.

In Chapter 3, we discussed about the four basic "meanings" that a family business can have. What the business "means" to the family has significant implications for not only dividend and reinvestment policy, but also the role of diversification in the business.

So how should family businesses think about diversification? When evaluating potential uses of capital, family business managers and directors should consider not just the expected return, but also the degree to which that return is correlated to the existing operations of the business. Depending on what the business "means" to the family, the potential for diversification benefits may take priority over absolute return. There are no right or wrong answers when it comes to risk tolerance, but there are tradeoffs that need to be acknowledged and communicated plainly. Family shareholders deserve to know not just the "what" but also the "why" for significant investment decisions.

Potential Next Steps

- ☐ Calculate what portion of the family's overall wealth is represented by the family business

- ☐ Identify the three biggest long-term strategic threats to the sustainability of the existing family business operations

- ☐ Establish a family LLC or partnership to hold a portfolio of diversifying assets (real estate, marketable securities, etc.)

- ☐ Create opportunities to provide seed funding to family members with compelling ideas for new business ventures

CHAPTER SIX

Does Father Always Know Best?

One of the greatest sources of strife in family businesses is ill-defined roles.

- What does a good shareholder do?

- What is expected of a family business director?

- How will the performance of management be evaluated?

Management accountability is hard for any company; effective management accountability within a complex web of family relationships can be an order of magnitude more difficult. Since some family members may fill multiple roles, clear and appropriate expectations paired with measurable outcomes are foundational to a management accountability structure that promotes business sustainability and family cohesion.

Who Sets Expectations?

Management accountability is an element of overall corporate governance. In family businesses, corporate governance and family governance can sometimes be hard to separate, but working to distinguish between the two pays dividends for both the business and the family.

The first step for many families in developing more formal governance is moving strategic business deliberations from the dining room to the board room. In the first generation, it is common for the board to consist only of mom and dad. As the business matures, the natural result of such arrangements is that the board meets continually, but never especially effectively. What works for the bootstrapping startup does not work for the established multi-generation family business. Formalizing the board governance process may be as simple as scheduling regular meetings, establishing appropriate sub-committees, and preparing real agendas which are distributed to directors prior to meetings. The addition of one or more independent directors may be appropriate for some family businesses. Independent directors with industry expertise and relevant experience can provide fresh perspective to deliberations and model how to provide frank feedback unencumbered by family baggage. The appointment of independent directors also signals that the board's job is company oversight, not to serve as the final arbiter for non-business family disputes.

> Since family businesses are free from the constraints of the quarterly reporting treadmill, management expectations should reflect the long-term goals that will promote the sustainability of the business and the financial success of the family.

A second common step is to establish a family council. While all family councils are unique, the principal role of the family council is to provide a forum for group decision-making on non-business family matters. Many family councils also provide opportunities for education regarding the business and collect input from family members about business decisions including dividend policy, capital structure, and capital budgeting (i.e., reinvestment). This input is valuable to the board, but is not binding; family business directors have sole responsibility for business oversight.

A parallel governance structure like that illustrated in Figure 8 helps to clarify that management (whether comprising family members or non-family professionals) is accountable to the board of directors, who in turn owe a fiduciary duty to the shareholders. As a result, the board of directors has the authority and responsibility to establish expectations for management, assess performance, and determine whether remedial actions are appropriate. In other

Figure 8

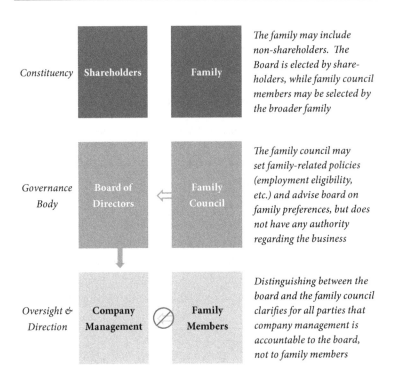

Constituency	**Shareholders**	**Family**	The family may include non-shareholders. The Board is elected by share-holders, while family council members may be selected by the broader family
Governance Body	**Board of Directors** ⇐	**Family Council**	The family council may set family-related policies (employment eligibility, etc.) and advise board on family preferences, but does not have any authority regarding the business
Oversight & Direction	**Company Management** ⊘	**Family Members**	Distinguishing between the board and the family council clarifies for all parties that company management is accountable to the board, not to family members

words, the CEO is accountable to the board of directors and not her obstreperous second cousin.

How Should Expectations Be Set?

One reason successful family businesses remain privately held is that such businesses can more easily avoid the "short-termism" perceived to afflict public markets, where success or failure might judged by next quarter's earnings release. Since family businesses are free from the constraints of the quarterly reporting treadmill, management expectations should reflect the long-term goals that will promote the sustainability of the business and the financial success of the family.

Developing a so-called "balanced scorecard" to evaluate management performance can help promote a long-term perspective that aligns management accountability with the overall health of the company. As developed by Professor Robert Kaplan of the Harvard Business School, a balanced scorecard can help promote management accountability by focusing on four key elements of business success.

- **Customer perspective**: How do customers see the business?

- **Internal business perspective**: What must the business excel at?

- **Innovation and learning perspective**: Can the business continue to improve and create value?

- **Financial perspective**: How does the business look to shareholders?

Notice that the financial perspective is only one component of the balanced scorecard. To be sure, if management succeeds with regard to the other perspectives, financial success should follow, but the idea is to take a broader view of corporate health, balancing traditional financial metrics with a few measurable operating metrics that will reveal whether the company is engaging in the activities that will promote the long-term sustainability (and financial performance) of the business.

> Management is accountable to the board of directors, not the family at large. Management performance should be evaluated relative to a set of clearly-defined and measurable objectives that further the long-term health and sustainability of the company.

The essence of a balanced scorecard—or any other management accountability tool—is pairing observable measures with business-specific goals under each perspective. Metrics that are not correlated to the company's strategies won't get traction, and goals that can't be measured won't be achieved. To be useful as a management accountability tool, the selected metrics should describe processes or outcomes over which management has at least some degree of control. For example, revenue per day of operation and number of rainout days are both measures that contribute to the financial success of a theme park, but only one is subject to management influence.

Making Accountability Work

Managing the family business is not a birthright, nor is it a responsibility that must be borne simply because of one's birth. It is a job, and the associated compensation and financial incentives should reflect market conditions. The hardest part of a management accountability system is deciding what to do when clearly-communicated goals are not met. An ill-conceived accountability framework that does not have the support of all the major stakeholders can—in the end—create more problems than it solves.

Goals may fail to be met for multiple reasons:

- **The goal was unrealistic.** In retrospect, it may be obvious that no management team could have delivered the specified results.

- **Management performed unsatisfactorily.** Given the available resources and prevailing market conditions, management simply failed to perform satisfactorily.

- **Market or other forces outside of management's control negatively affected the business.** Going back to our prior example, the theme park may have suffered through an abnormally rainy summer.

- **The business strategy proved to be ineffective and needs to be revised.** Management has executed the plan flawlessly, but the plan did not accurately reflect the customer, supplier, technological, or competitive forces shaping the industry.

The reasons for failure are not always easy to discern. If the goals were unrealistic, management accountability should look different than if management performed unsatisfactorily. If the business strategy proved to be ineffective, who was responsible for developing the strategy? If the board supported, or perhaps even mandated, the strategy, to what degree should management be accountable for its failure? Evaluating management performance requires both strong nerves and the ability be flexible when warranted. A seasoned, independent outside voice on the board can be especially valuable when poor performance needs to be evaluated.

Conclusion

Management accountability in family businesses is hard. Overlooking the failures of a favored relative and magnifying minor faults because of a strained family relationship are both ever-present temptations. In the end, management is accountable to the board of directors, not the family at large. Management performance should be evaluated relative to a set of clearly-defined and measurable objectives that further the long-term health and sustainability of the company. Evaluating management performance when goals are not met is difficult, but failing to evaluate performance (and thereby letting problems fester) is not a responsible course of action.

Potential Next Steps

- ☐ Identify potential candidates for independent (non-family) board members
- ☐ Establish a family council
- ☐ Develop a balanced scorecard for evaluating management performance
- ☐ Design management incentives that align with the components of the balanced scorecard
- ☐ Create a board committee responsible for periodic formal review of management performance

CHAPTER SEVEN

How Do We Find Our Next Leader?

Next Man (or Woman) Up?

Perhaps no group is as proficient at the art of clichéd answers as football coaches. When confronted with the season-ending injury of a star player, the coach will inevitably stare stoically into the camera and solemnly declare "Next man up." Whether the coach truly believes that the replacement player will be adequate, the cliché is intended to convey the idea that the coach has created such a "culture of success" or "Process" (two of the newer clichés) that the team's performance will be unaffected.

From the perspective of family business, "Next Man or Woman Up" is one approach that directors can take to management succession. Perhaps for some family businesses, management succession is as simple as pulling the next available candidate from the management depth chart. But we suspect that approach falls short for most family businesses. The combination of business growth, generational dynamics, and intra-family relationships that make family businesses unique precludes one-size-fits-all solutions to management succession. The primary questions associated with management succession are (1) Who will be the next leader of the business? and (2) How will the transition occur?

First Question: Who?

In our experience, many succession struggles are rooted in a failure to distinguish between being a good family member, a good employee, and a good business leader. The combination of native ability, education, character, social IQ, technical skills, and strategic savvy necessary to run a large business successfully is rare. The often-unspoken assumption that, since Dick has been a good son, or Jane a good daughter, he or she is entitled to run the business when his or her turn comes up is unfair to the shareholders and employees of the business, not to mention Dick or Jane. While there are abundant examples of capable and energetic second, third or later generation family members that are great business leaders, it is a mistake to think that management of the business should simply be a matter of inheritance.

The second common myth is that since Bill and Suzie have demonstrated themselves to be great employees (in whatever functional area) that they will therefore be great leaders. Being good at one's job does not guarantee success as the leader of a family business. Further, as companies grow, new challenges may require a different set of leadership skills than were required in the prior generation. The skills and personality traits that made Uncle Phil the ideal leader of the business twenty-five years ago may be different from what Cousin Carlton needs to possess for success in the same role today.

> It is a mistake to think that management of the business should simply be a matter of inheritance.

If the family has successfully distinguished family membership from family business management, it may be easier for the board to cast a wider net to find the best candidate to assume leadership of the business. Having an "outside" CEO does not mean the company has ceased to be a family business any more than hiring the first non-family employee on the shop floor did. Rather, it simply means that the directors have fulfilled their responsibilities to shareholders, employees and the community by seeking the right candidate for the job. Family members are by no means ruled out from consideration, but directors must acknowledge that the requisite skills may not reside in the family. And that's okay. Having "professional" management may actually help family cohesion and, therefore, business sustainability.

In many cases, the combination of outside perspective and family loyalty that make a successful leader can be found among the family's in-laws. Such "married-ins" are often sufficiently removed from family dynamics that they can see business issues for what they are, uncolored by what may be decades' worth of emotional baggage. At the same time, their membership in the family may give a head-start in aligning economic incentives. In other words, "married-ins" will likely have plenty of skin in the game.

Second Question: How?

In the long run, management succession is inevitable: the proportion of managers that are eventually replaced is 100%. In the short run, however, there are generally three circumstances giving rise to management succession.

1. **Planned Retirement.** When the senior executive is approaching a natural retirement age, the directors should identify potential candidates to replace the retiring leader. With a multi-year planning horizon, the board can give due consideration to family candidates, develop mentoring opportunities for those candidates, and evaluate performance of those candidates in areas of increasing responsibility. If it becomes apparent that no family candidates represent the right fit for the job, the board can extend the search to include both existing non-family employees and non-employees.

    The appropriate retirement age for family business executives is a vexing issue. There simply is no one-size-fits-all point at which a successful family business leader should step away. In our practice, we have seen examples of departures that—in hindsight—were premature, because the designated replacement was not yet ready to assume leadership. Perhaps more commonly, we see examples of businesses that plateau and stagnate because an aging senior executive refuses to move out of the corner office.

2. **Performance-Driven Transition.** We wrote in the prior chapter about the unique challenges associated with management accountability in family businesses. If the directors determine an existing senior executive is not generating acceptable results, it may be appropriate to seek

a replacement. Family dynamics can make this an extremely difficult decision, and the prospect that such a decision may be in the best interest of the principal stakeholders (family shareholders, employees, local community, customers, suppliers, etc.) is one good reason to include qualified independent non-family members on the board. The independent directors can provide an objective assessment of managerial performance uncolored by internal family dynamics. If a performance-driven transition is necessary, the ultimate replacement should not be selected hastily; the long-run health of the business may be better served by a deliberate selection process, during which an experienced executive can manage the company on an interim basis.

3. **Unexpected Vacancy.** Finally, management succession may be forced upon the company because of an untimely illness, death, or other unforeseen circumstances. No business is immune to such circumstances, which underscores the need for directors to think proactively about management succession, even when the current leader is successful and expected to have a lengthy remaining tenure. When tragedy strikes, selecting the next leader should still be considered a measure-twice, cut-once project, with the long-term health of the organization taking precedence over the short-term desire to fill the position.

As noted in the *Harvard Business Review,* recent research by Stephanie Querbach, Miriam Bird, and Nadine Kammerlander offers some interesting insights into best practices for management succession in family businesses. After studying over 500 management successions, they concluded the likelihood that successor-managers would be able to implement needed changes and improve the long-term sustainability of the family business was linked to three strategies: (1) limiting the power of the outgoing CEO subsequent to his or her retirement, (2) crafting a formal agreement regarding the how and when of power transfer, and (3) selecting a non-family successor. Of course, these observations reflect probabilities—they're not absolute prescriptions for how every succession should occur. But they do provide a somewhat counter-intuitive perspective on the topic that family businesses would do well to consider.

In the end, every management succession plan will be as unique as the family business it is designed for. But one constant for all family businesses is that now is the time to begin thinking and planning. "Next Man Up" may work in football, but your family business deserves better.

Potential Next Steps

- ☐ Create an organization chart that identifies current leaders and existing management "depth" at each position

- ☐ Identify the qualities/attributes needed for the next generation of leaders to be successful

- ☐ Evaluate strengths and capabilities of the rising generation of managers (current family employees, current non-family employees, and non-employee family members)

- ☐ Establish a timeline for the planned retirement of existing senior managers

- ☐ Identify what ongoing role former managers will have in the business

CHAPTER EIGHT

Is There a Ticking Time Bomb Lurking in Our Family Business?

When we talk with family business owners, most confess a vague recollection of having signed a buy-sell agreement, but only a few can give a clear and concise overview of the agreement's key terms. Yet no other governing document has such potentially profound implications for the business and for the family. My colleague of nearly 20 years, Chris Mercer, literally wrote the book(s) when it comes to buy-sell agreements (*Buy-Sell Agreements for Closely Held and Family Business Owners*, Peabody Publishing, 2010). Chris and I recently sat down to talk about buy-sell agreements in the context of family businesses.

Travis: Chris, to start off, what is the purpose of a buy-sell agreement? Why should a family business have one?

Chris: A buy-sell agreement ensures that the owners of a business will have as fellow-owners only those individuals who are acceptable to the group. A buy-sell agreement formalizes agreements in the present—while everyone is alive and well—regarding how future transactions will occur, with respect to both pricing and terms, when the agreement is "triggered."

Every business with two or more owners should have a buy-sell agreement, and that includes family businesses. What I can tell you, after many years of working with companies and their buy-sell agreements, is that once an agreement is triggered—for example, by the death, disability or departure of a shareholder—the interests of the departed and remaining shareholders diverge. When interests diverge, an agreement is virtually impossible even, or especially, within families. So, a well-crafted buy-sell agreement establishes an agreement in advance, so the family can avoid problems and conflict in the future.

Travis: The title of your first book on buy-sell agreements described them as either reasonable resolutions or ticking time bombs. How could a buy-sell agreement become a ticking time bomb for a family business?

Chris: Sure—here's a quick example. Some agreements specify a fixed price for shares that the shareholders have all agreed to. The price is binding until updated to a new agreed-upon price. The idea sounds good in principle, but in reality, the owners almost never agree on an updated price. Years later, after a substantial increase in a company's value renders the agreed-upon price stale, a trigger event occurs. The ticking time bomb explodes on the departing shareholder who receives an inadequate price for their shares. A second explosion occurs with the ensuing litigation to try to "fix" the problem. Needless to say, I do not recommend the use of fixed-price valuation mechanisms in buy-sell agreements.

Travis: Buy-sell agreements often define a formula for determining value when triggered. Can a "formula price" provide for a reasonable resolution?

> Your family's buy-sell agreement won't matter until it does, and then, it will be the only thing that matters.

Chris: Travis, I've said many times that some owners and advisers search for the perfect formula like the Knights Templar sought the Holy Grail. The perfect formula does not exist. Given changes in the company over time, evolving industry conditions, emerging competition, and changes in the availability of financing, no formula will remain reasonable over time. It is simply not possible to anticipate all the factors an experienced business appraiser would consider at a future date. All this assumes that the formula is understandable. Some formulas in buy-sell agreements are written so obtusely that reasonable people reach (potentially quite) different results. As you might suspect, I do not recommend the use of formula pricing mechanisms in buy-sell agreements.

Travis: Other agreements provide for an appraisal process upon a trigger event. What are the benefits or pitfalls of such appraisal processes?

Chris: The most common appraisal process found in buy-sell agreements calls for the use of two or three appraisers to determine the price to be paid if and when a trigger event occurs. One of the biggest problems out of the gate is that no one knows what the price of their shares will be until the end of a lengthy and potentially disastrous appraisal process.

Let me explain. Assume that the shareholders have agreed on an appraisal process to determine price upon a trigger event. The Company retains one appraiser and the selling shareholder retains a second. Far too often, the language describing the type of value for the appraisers to determine is vague and inconsistent. The selling shareholder's appraiser interprets value as an undiscounted strategic value, say $100 per share. The company's appraiser interprets the same language as calling for significant minority interest and marketability discounts and concludes a value of, say, $40 per share. The agreement calls for the two appraisers to agree on a third appraiser who is supposed to resolve the issue. How? The two positions are not reconcilable. Litigation, unhappiness, wasted time and expense follow as the time bomb, which has been in place for years, explodes on all the parties.

Travis: So if fixed price, formula price, and appraisal process agreements all have serious drawbacks, what kind of pricing mechanism do you recommend for most family businesses?

Chris: Based on my experiences over many years, I have concluded that the best pricing mechanism for most family businesses is what I call a "Single Appraiser, Select Now and Value Now" valuation process. The parties agree on a single appraiser (I'd recommend Mercer Capital, of course!). The selected appraiser provides a valuation now, at the time of selection, based on the language in the buy-sell agreement. This ensures that any confusion is eliminated at the time of signing or revision. The appraisal sets the price for the buy-sell agreement until the next (preferably annual) appraisal. With this kind of process, virtually all of the problems we've discussed are eliminated, or reduced substantially. All the shareholders know what the current value is at any time. Importantly, they all know the process that will occur with every subsequent appraisal. The certainty provided by this "Single Appraiser, Select Now and Value Now" process far outweighs the uncertainty inherent in other processes at a reasonable cost. At Mercer Capital, we provide annual appraisals of over 100 companies for buy-sell agreements and other purposes.

Travis: Finally, what is your best piece of advice for family business owners when it comes to buy-sell agreements?

Chris: The best advice I have for family business owners is to be sure that there is agreement regarding their buy-sell agreements. Many companies have had agreements in place for many years, often decades, without any changes or revisions. No one knows what will happen if they are triggered. Agreement regarding a buy-sell agreement should be the result of review by all shareholders, corporate counsel, and, I recommend, a qualified business appraiser. The appraiser should review agreements from business and valuation perspectives to be sure that the valuation mechanism will work when it is triggered. Discussions are not always easy, since shareholders from different generations and different branches of the family tree have differing objectives and viewpoints. Yet if all parties can agree now, the family can avoid unnecessary strife and litigation in the future. So the best advice I have is to "Just Do It!"

Conclusion

Your family's buy-sell agreement won't matter until it does. As families prepare for their next business meeting, leaders should carefully consider putting a review of the buy-sell agreement on the agenda.

Potential Next Steps

- ☐ Read the family business buy-sell agreement and distribute copies to shareholders

- ☐ Assess valuation mechanism in the existing buy-sell agreement: Is it understandable? Does it align with the shareholders' objectives if a triggering event occurs?

- ☐ Identify a qualified, independent business appraiser to use in valuing the business

- ☐ Measure the current value of the business for purposes of the buy-sell agreement

CHAPTER NINE

What Is the Family's Most Valuable Asset?

In April 2018, European investment banking icon Rothschild & Co. announced that 37-year old Alexandre de Rothschild would be taking the reins at the firm, succeeding his father at the bank's May 2018 shareholders' meeting. The new chairman is a member of the seventh generation of the family. While the future performance of the bank under the younger Mr. Rothschild will be the ultimate barometer of success, the Rothschild family clearly has fostered a culture of intentionally developing the next generation. Few families have the long history of next-gen development that the Rothschild's do, but it is a task that becomes more important with each successive generation. The long-term health of any organization ultimately depends on the quality of the rising generation of leaders, and families are no different.

From our experience working with successful family businesses, talking with family business leaders, and reviewing relevant research, we've identified themes that are common to successful family businesses when it comes to developing the next generation of shareholders:

- **Successful families recognize that each succeeding generation will be different, and that's okay.** As families mature and grow, succeeding generations naturally become more diffuse than their parents' generation. Family members move away, pursue careers and interests outside the family business, and have different personal and financial objectives. While this increasing family diversity can be intimidating, successful families embrace the new experiences, opportunities, and challenges that this growth brings. Imposing obligations on the next generation to do things just like grand-dad did generally prove to be stifling and counter-productive (and, in all likelihood, contrary to grand-dad's mindset when he was achieving his greatest business successes). The differences between Boomers, Gen Xers, and Millennials are real and matter for family businesses. Groups like the Center for Generational Kinetics publish fascinating research on the differences between generations and how to make those differences productive for your family and business.

- **Successful families identify the core business and family attributes that the family wants to persist across generations.** This is the counter-weight to the prior theme: families have "social ballast" that can help the business maintain its balance in the inevitable rough seas. This "social ballast" comprises the core family and business attributes that maintain and preserve identity across generational changes. The key is to identify the root causes of the family's success. Without saddling the next generation with a mandate to do things just like grand-dad did, can the family identify the core attributes underlying grand-dad's success that can transcend generations? For example, what are the two or three core attributes that make a Rothschild business a Rothschild business? Identifying these attributes does not limit the next generation's flexibility, but rather frees the next generation from having to develop—out of whole cloth—a framework within which to meet the unique family and business challenges with which it will be faced.

- **Successful families acknowledge that experiences outside the family business promote development of next generation leaders.** While growing up in the family business provides development opportunities that are not easily replicated, many successful families are recognizing the benefit of gaining professional experiences outside the family business. Family employment policies often mandate that before becoming eligible to work in the business, family members must have three to five (or more) years of external professional experience. Such policies have multiple potential benefits, not least of which is exposing the next generation to the ideas, processes, and strategies of other successful businesses. As noted in the article mentioned above, the younger Mr. Rothschild spent the first five years of his career working at other financial firms before joining the family business. Furthermore, even in the context of non-employee roles (shareholder, family council member, director), successful families value and encourage the "outside" experiences of the next generation.

- **Successful families provide development opportunities for both employee and non-employee shareholders.** Regardless of the current family composition, the likelihood that rising generations will include a mix of employee and non-employee shareholders is high. Next generation development is not limited to future employees, but should include members of the rising generation that do not plan to work in the business. Development opportunities include both education and service. No one is born knowing what has made the family business successful, how to read the company's financial statements, or how to think about the tradeoffs between current distributions and investment for future growth. Suc-

> If the current generation of business leaders is focused on the long-term sustainability and health of the family business, developing the next generation of family shareholders must be viewed as a strategic priority.

cessful families are intentional about providing ongoing education on these and other topics for the next generation. With regard to service, rotating membership on a family council can create great opportunities for non-employee members of the next generation to actively contribute to the success of the family.

- **Successful families allocate resources to fostering next generation innovations.** The next generation is a natural source of innovation necessary to keep the family business relevant in evolving markets.

Successful families consider multiple potential strategies for accomplishing this goal. Some families follow a corporate venture capital model, providing seed capital to fund new ventures headed by members of the next generation (subject, of course, to rigorous vetting procedures). If there is some organic connection between the proposed venture and the family's core operations, such investments may be made by the family business itself. If the proposed venture is a bit further afield, a holding company structure may be used to make the investment. Or, if the risk-return preferences of various family members do not all accommodate venture investing, the family may explore setting up a captive venture fund in which family members may, but are not obliged to, invest. Still other companies view significant ongoing distributions as the seed money for the next generation to put into new ventures of their own choosing.

- **Successful families use philanthropy as a tool in next generation development.** Perhaps the most effective way to develop the next generation is to provide for active involvement in the family's philanthropic efforts. Having a voice in the family's giving and other charitable activities can be a great way for the next generation of the family to develop a sense of the responsibility for managing and stewarding the wealth created by prior generations for the benefit of their communities and other worthy beneficiaries. For many families, this is such an important component of developing the next generation that they include even teens and pre-teens in their philanthropic efforts.

At the risk of sounding overly sentimental, a family's most valuable asset is its next generation. If the current generation of business leaders is focused on the long-term sustainability and health of the family business, developing the next generation of family shareholders must be viewed as a strategic priority.

Potential Next Steps

☐ Identify the core business and family attributes that need to persist across generations

☐ Develop a family employment policy, including requirements for professional experience outside the family business

☐ Identify education, service, and philanthropic opportunities for the rising generation of family members (both employees and non-employees)

☐ Establish a family venture fund to foster next generation innovations

CHAPTER TEN

What Should We Do About Estate Taxes?

Family business owners cite different motives for investing their time, energy, and savings to build successful businesses. Some have entrepreneurial zeal, while others are creators who see problems in the world that they can solve. Others are natural leaders who are inspired by the job opportunities and other "positive externalities" that successful enterprises generate for employees and the communities in which they operate. But common to nearly all family business owners is the desire to provide financially for their heirs. As a result, one of the most common concerns such owners cite is the ability to transfer ownership of the family business to the next generation in the most tax-efficient way.

The IRS defines the estate tax as the: "...tax on your right to transfer property at your death." The amount of tax is calculated with reference to the decedent's gross estate, which is the sum of the fair market value of the decedent's assets less certain deductions for mortgages/debts, the value of property passing to a spouse or charity, and the costs of administering the estate.

As with all taxes, things are not as simple as they seem. Before calculating the estate tax due, two adjustments are made. First, all taxable gifts previously made by the decedent (and therefore no longer in the estate) are added to the gross estate. Second, the sum of the gross estate and prior taxable gifts is reduced by the available unified credit. The unified credit for 2018 is just over $11 million. Figure 9 illustrates the calculations for the taxable estate of an unmarried individual.

Figure 9

Fair Market Value of Decedent's Assets	$35,000,000
less: Mortgages and Other Debts	(6,500,000)
less: Amounts Passing to Spouse	0
less: Amounts to be Received by Charity	(2,500,000)
less: Estate Administration Expenses	(150,000)
Gross Estate	$25,850,000
plus: Taxable Gifts Made During Lifetime	4,500,000
less: Available Unified Credit	(11,180,000)
Taxable Amount	$19,170,000
times: Estate Tax Rate	40%
Estate Tax Due	$7,668,000

To complicate things a bit further, estates have benefited from the introduction of "portability" to the estate tax regime in 2011. Portability refers to the ability of an individual to transfer the unused portion of their available unified credit to a surviving spouse. The ultimate effect of portability is that for married family business owners, the total available unified credit is slightly more than $22 million.

Taxes are never fun, but what proves to be especially vexing about the estate tax for family business owners is that a substantial portion of their estate often consists of illiquid interests in private company stock. Going back for a moment to our prior example, if the decedent's assets consist primarily of a portfolio of marketable securities, it is relatively easy to liquidate a portion of the portfolio to fund payment of the tax. If, on the other hand, the decedent's assets are primarily in the form of shares in the family business, liquidating assets to pay the estate tax may prove more difficult (estate taxes are payable in cash and may not be paid in-kind with family business shares). As a result, family businesses may be sold or be forced to borrow money to fund payment of a decedent's estate tax liability.

Attorneys who specialize in estate taxes have devised numerous strategies for helping families manage estate tax obligations. Strategies range from relatively simple, such as a program of regular gifts to family members, to complex, such as the use of specialized trusts. While the finer points of various potential strategies is beyond the scope of this chapter, the concept of fair market value is essential to understanding and evaluating any estate planning strategy.

> The fair market value of family business shares in an estate depends not just on the fundamentals of the business but also on the relevant level of value.

What is Fair Market Value?

As noted above, fair market value is the standard of value for measuring the decedent's estate, and therefore, the estate tax due. The IRS's estate tax regulations define fair market value as "the price at which the property would change hands between a willing buyer and a willing seller, neither being under any compulsion to buy or to sell and both having reasonable knowledge of relevant facts."

So far, so good.

But how does all this work for a family business? To understand the underlying rationale for much estate planning, we need to explore how the standard of value intersects with what is referred to as the level of value. In other words, the fair market value of family business shares in an estate depends not just on the fundamentals of the business (expected future revenues, profits, investment needs, risk, etc.) but also on the relevant level of value.

If an estate owns a controlling interest in a family business (in most cases, more than 50% of the stock), the fair market value of those shares will reflect the estate's ability to sell the business to a competitor, supplier, customer, or financially-motivated buyer such as a private equity fund. In contrast, the owner of a small minority block of the outstanding shares of a family business has no ability to force the business to change strategy, seek a sale of the business, or otherwise unilaterally compel any action. As a result, the owner of the shares is limited to waiting until the shareholders that do have control decide to sell the business or redeem the minority investor's shares. In the meantime, they wait (and, potentially, collect dividends). If there is a willing buyer for the shares, they may elect to sell, but that buyer will be subject to the same illiquidity, holding period risks, and uncertainties, so the price is unlikely to be attractive.

Business appraisers often describe the levels of value with reference to a chart like Figure 10.

Figure 10

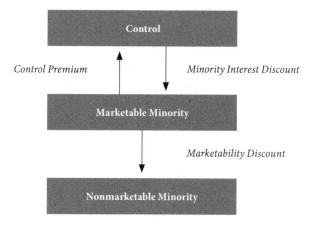

The levels of value chart captures two essentially common-sense notions regarding value. First, investors prefer to have control rather than not. The degree to which control is valuable will depend on a whole host of case-specific facts and circumstances, but in general, having control is preferred. Second, investors prefer liquidity to illiquidity. Again, the magnitude of the appropriate marketability discount will depend on specific factors, but not surprisingly, investors prefer to have a ready market for their shares. Fair market value is measured with respect to both of these common-sense notions.

Estate Planning Objectives

As a result, one objective of most estate planning techniques is to ensure—through whatever particular mechanism—that no individual owns a controlling interest in the family business at his or her death. Of course, minimizing taxes is only one possible objective of an estate planning process, which might include asset protection, business continuity, and providing for loved ones.

Therefore, family businesses should carefully consider whether an estate planning strategy designed to minimize estate taxes will have any unintended negative consequences for the business or the family.

- For example, an aggressive gifting program that causes the founder to relinquish control prematurely may increase the likelihood of intra-family strife, or jeopardize the family's ability to make timely strategic decisions on behalf of the business.

- Or, adoption of an unusually restrictive redemption policy in an effort to minimize the fair market value of minority shares in the company may lead to inequitable outcomes for family members having a legitimate need to sell shares.

In short, families should be careful not to let the tax tail wag the business dog. Families should consult legal, accounting, and valuation advisors who understand their business needs, family dynamics, and objectives to ensure that their estate plan accomplishes the desired goals.

Potential Next Steps

- ☐ Review the current shareholder list / ownership structure for the family business

- ☐ Identify current estate tax exposures and develop a funding plan for meeting those obligations when they arise

- ☐ Identify tax and non-tax goals of the estate planning process

- ☐ Obtain a current opinion of the fair market value of the business at each level of value (control, marketable minority, and nonmarketable minority)

CHAPTER ELEVEN

How Should We Respond to an Acquisition Offer?

Successful businesses don't have to go looking for potential acquirers—potential acquirers are likely to come looking for them. Most of our family business clients have no intention of selling in the near-term, and yet they often receive a steady stream of unsolicited offers from eager suitors. Many of these offers can be quickly dismissed as uninformed or bottom-fishing, but serious inquiries from legitimate buyers of capacity occasionally appear that require a response.

What Kinds of Buyers are There?

Buyers are generally classified into two categories.

- **Financial buyers** are groups like private equity funds that purchase businesses with a view toward earning a return on their investment over a finite holding period. These buyers generally use financial leverage to magnify their returns, and expect to exit their investment by selling the business to another buyer after three to seven (or maybe even ten) years. While financial buyers may have specific plans for making the business run more efficiently and profitably, they are generally not anticipating significant revenue synergies or expense savings from wholesale changes to the business. Rather, they tend to be more focused on incremental changes to boost value and clever financial engineering to be the principal engines driving their returns.

- **Strategic buyers** are competitors, customers, or suppliers of the business who have a strategic goal for making the acquisition. Such buyers certainly want to earn a return on their investment, but that return is expected to come from combining the target's operations with their own, rather than through financial engineering. In other words, strategic buyers look to long-term value creation through assimilating the target into their existing business, not a short-term return from buying low and selling high. Strategic buyers may anticipate revenue synergies through the combination or may foresee the opportunity to eliminate operating expenses in either the acquired or legacy businesses to fuel cash flow growth.

Distinguishing between financial and strategic buyers is important for evaluating unsolicited offers, but we suspect that a more important distinction is that between motivated buyers and opportunistic buyers. Successful family businesses will attract motivated buyers who have the capacity to pay an attractive price for the business, but should strive to avoid opportunistic buyers who are seeking to take advantage of some temporary market dislocation or cyclical weakness to get the business at a depressed price.

Evaluating Acquisition Offers

Evaluating acquisition offers is ultimately the duty of the board of directors, not the family at large. Uncle Charlie may have strong opinions on the proposed deal, but if he is not a director, he does not have the responsibility or authority to respond to the offer. That does not mean that the directors will not care about Uncle Charlie's perspective. As we've discussed, it is critical for the board to understand what the business "means" to the family, and the meaning of the business to the family may well inform how the directors evaluate the offer. For larger families, the prospect of receiving a potentially attractive unsolicited acquisition offer underscores the value of a regular survey process, whereby the board and senior management periodically take the pulse of the family on topics at the intersection of business and family.

Family business directors should evaluate offers along several dimensions:

- **Buyer Motivation.** What has prompted the offer? If it is a strategic acquirer, what sort of operational changes would be expected post-transaction? Will a sale result in facility closures, administrative layoffs, or discontinuation of the business name? Or, could the sale increase opportunities for employees and expose the brand to new markets? If the suitor is a financial buyer, what sort of debt load will they place on the company post-acquisition? Will the company's ability to withstand normal economic downturns be compromised? Will the buyer want members of the family active in senior management to continue to run the business? The answers to these and similar questions should be considered in the context of what the business means to the family and help inform whether the offer should be entertained further.

- **Buyer Capacity.** Does the buyer have the financial capacity to actually execute the transaction if it is agreed to? If external financing is required, will it be available to the buyer when needed? Basic due diligence goes both ways. Going through a lengthy negotiation and due diligence process only to have the transaction fall apart at the closing table due to lack of financing will leave a bad taste in the family's mouth.

- **Price & Transaction Structure.** What seems on the surface to be an attractive price may, upon further examination, turn out to be a far less attractive transaction. A sale of stock may have a lower nominal price than a sale of assets, yet result in higher after-tax proceeds. A high nominal price may be subject to contingencies regarding future performance which cause the economic value of the offer to be far less. Or, a high nominal price may be payable, in part, in shares of the buyer rather than cash—what is the family's appetite for trading stock in the family business for stock in a different business over which they will likely have no control? There are many other components of transaction structure, such as required representations and warranties or escrow provisions that can significantly influence how attractive an offer really is.

- **Price is not everything.** Just because the price is adequate and the terms are acceptable does not mean that the timing is optimal for a sale. Directors should carefully weigh the potential outcomes for shareholders by deferring a transaction: Is the family better served by taking the bird in hand or waiting for more birds to materialize in the bush?

If the company is on a growth trajectory or has its own acquisition opportunities to pursue, it may command a larger multiple down the road. Understanding the risks and opportunities associated with the timing of a transaction requires directors to be well-attuned to company, market, and industry dynamics. Family directors-in-name-only are unlikely to have anything meaningful to add to such deliberations.

- **Reinvestment Opportunities.** Does the family have a plan for putting sale proceeds to work? Once again, what the business "means" to the family comes to the fore. Will proceeds simply be distributed to the various branches of the family, to use or invest as they see fit? Or will proceeds be retained at the family level and redeployed in other assets for the benefit of the family? If so, are there reinvestment opportunities available that will "fit" the cash flow needs and risk tolerances of the family? Will such investments provide the same degree of family cohesion as the legacy business? A sale of the family business may have unintended, and potentially far-reaching consequences for the family.

Responding to Acquisition Offers

Once the board has evaluated the unsolicited offer, there are essentially four responses to choose from:

- **Reject the offer.** If the directors conclude that the proposed price and/ or terms are unattractive, or if the timing of a transaction does not align with the broader goals of the family, the board may elect simply to reject the offer.

- **Negotiate with the potential acquirer.** If the directors conclude that the timing is right and that the suitor would be an attractive acquirer, the board may elect to negotiate with the buyer with a view toward consummating a transaction. If the perceived "fit" between the family business and the potential acquirer is good, proceeding directly to negotiating price and terms of the transaction may result in the quickest and smoothest path to close. However, without any exposure to the market, there is a risk that the negotiated price and terms are not really optimal. There is a reason private equity firms like to tout their "proprietary" deal flow to potential investors—direct negotiation with sellers presumably results in lower purchase prices than winning auctions does.

- **Engage in a limited sale process.** Given the potential for underpayment, directors may elect to discreetly contact a limited number of other potential acquirers to gauge their interest in making a competing bid for the business. The benefit of doing a limited market check is that it can generally be done fairly quickly without "putting the company up for sale" with the attendant publicity that the family may not desire. The initial suitor will, of course, generally prefer that even a limited sale process not be engaged in, and may seek some sort of exclusivity provision which precludes the seller from talking to other potential buyers. Directors will need to consider carefully whether the potential benefits of a limited sale process will outweigh the risk that such a process will cause the initial suitor to rescind their offer and walk away.

- **Engage in a full sale process/auction.** Finally, the board may conclude as a result of their deliberations that the unsolicited offer signals that it is an opportune time to sell the business because pricing and terms are expected to

> Most family businesses have no intention of selling; however, when a legitimate, unsolicited offer arrives, what do you do?

be favorable in the market and the family's circumstances align well with a sale. In a full sale process, the company's financial advisors will prepare a descriptive investment memorandum for distribution to a carefully vetted list of potential motivated acquirers. After initial indications of interest are received, the universe of potential buyers is then narrowed to a manageable group of interested parties who are invited to view presentations by senior management and engage in limited due diligence with a view to making a formal bid for the business. With the help of their financial advisors, the directors evaluate the bids with regard to pricing, terms, and cultural fit, selecting a company with which to negotiate a definitive purchase agreement and close the transaction. A full sale process will likely involve the most time and expense, and may expose to competitors the family's intention to sell, but carries with it the potential for achieving the most favorable price and terms.

Bringing Together the Right Team

There is a sharp experience imbalance in most transactions: buyers have often completed many transactions, while sellers may have never sold a business before. As a result, sellers need to assemble a team of experienced and trusted advisors to help them navigate the unfamiliar terrain. The transaction team will include at least three primary players: a transaction attorney, a tax accountant, and a financial advisor.

Definitive purchase agreements are long, complicated contracts, and an experienced attorney is essential to memorializing the substantive terms of the transaction in the agreement and ensuring that the sellers' legal interests are fully protected.

Business transactions also have significant tax consequences, and the tax code is arcane and littered with pitfalls for the unwary. Trusting the buyer to do your tax homework can be a very costly mistake. An experienced tax attorney is essential to maximizing after-tax proceeds to the family.

The financial advisor takes the lead in helping the board evaluate unsolicited offers, setting value expectations, preparing the descriptive information memorandum, identifying a target list of potential motivated buyers of capacity, assessing initial indications of interest and formal bids, facilitating due diligence, and negotiating key economic terms of the definitive agreement. My colleague Nick Heinz leads Mercer Capital's transaction advisory practice, and Nick likes to say that his job in a transaction is to run the transaction on behalf of the company so the company's management can focus on running the business on behalf of the shareholders. Transactions can be time-consuming and mentally draining, and it's simply not possible for company management to devote the necessary time to managing the transaction process and the business at the same time. An experienced financial advisor takes that burden off of management.

When it comes to assembling the right team, business owners sometimes blanch at the cost. However, the cost of a quality and experienced team of advisors pales next to the cost of fumbling on the transaction. The family will only sell the business once, and there are no do-overs. As we recently heard someone say, "Cheap expertise is an oxymoron."

Potential Next Steps

- ☐ Gauge family members' appetite for a sale of the business
- ☐ Identify the attributes of an acquirer to whom the family would be willing to sell the business
- ☐ Identify steps that can be taken to improve the "curb appeal" of the family business
- ☐ Assess reinvestment opportunities for the family in the event of a sale
- ☐ Interview potential financial advisors that can help the family evaluate offers and execute transactions

CHAPTER TWELVE

Who's In and
Who's Out?

As family businesses evolve, the family's leaders need to determine the appropriate relationship between membership in the family and ownership in the business. As the third, fourth, and subsequent generations of the family reach adulthood, it becomes increasingly likely that the interests of at least some family members will diverge from the interests of the business.

Family businesses can adopt one of two broad strategies to address this situation:

1. Maintain broad-based ownership and make positive shareholder engagement a strategic priority; or,

2. Use share redemptions and liquidity programs to achieve concentrated ownership among a subset of the family.

Neither strategy is inherently superior to the other. We discussed the benefits (and challenges) of developing positive shareholder engagement in Chapter 1. In this chapter, we focus on the second strategy.

Motivations for Selling Shares

In this chapter, we focus on voluntary, rather than involuntary, sales of shares. Involuntary sales of shares include those triggered by, and governed by, the relevant terms of the company's buy-sell agreement. Chapter 8 provides a brief overview of the issues associated with buy-sell agreements.

In some families, selling shares in the family business is perceived as nothing short of treason. Yet, there are often legitimate reasons for family members to sell shares in the family business, such as a desire for diversification, proceeds to start a new business venture, or funding education or other major life events.

In our experience, the desire of family shareholders for liquidity (whether full or partial) can usually be traced to some form of "clientele" effect. The clientele effect names the fact that a company's shareholder base is not monolithic: different shareholders have different portfolios, risk preferences, income needs, and expectations. In multi-generation family businesses, we find the clientele effect to be common. As the family grows numerically and spreads out geographically and occupationally, it is only natural for shareholders no longer to look so much alike. Differing shareholder needs and preferences are not wrong, but when treated as such, the resulting suspicion can lead to resentment, open conflict, and in too many cases, litigation.

Shareholder clienteles can form along many different potential axes: kinship, geography, employment status, etc. To illustrate the concept, consider the economic role the family business can fulfill in different households, as depicted in Figure 11.

It is only natural that family members in the upper right quadrant view the family business very differently from their cousins or siblings in the lower left quadrant. Those in the upper right quadrant are likely to be very risk-averse, desiring preservation of capital and the current level of dividends above all else. Shareholders in the lower left quadrant will much more closely resemble public market investors, supporting corporate strategies that enhance returns at acceptable risk levels.

For public companies, the clientele effect sorts itself out because shareholders self-select; if the attributes of the company don't align a shareholders preferences and risk tolerances, it is very easy for the shareholder to sell their holdings and find assets that are a better fit. For family businesses, however, things are not nearly so tidy.

Faced with multiple shareholder clienteles, family business leaders can seek to adopt distribution and reinvestment policies that accommodate as many shareholders as possible. Or, the family can adopt a formal share redemption or liquidity program with a view to providing shareholders greater flexibility in

Figure 11

Illustration of Clientele Effect Among Family Business Shareholders

Family Business as % of Total Wealth

	Low	*Wealth Concentration*	*High*

		Low	High
Dividends as % of Total Income	High	Diversified Wealth, but Income Dependence	Concentrated Wealth, with Income Dependence
	Income Concentration	Fully Diversified	Concentrated Wealth, but Income Independence
	Low		

tailoring the economic benefits of family membership to the unique circumstances of their particular household.

Elements of a Shareholder Liquidity Program

While every shareholder liquidity program is unique, there are certain structural elements that all plans, whether formal or informal, must have.

Buyer

There has to be a source for the liquidity made available to selling shareholders. The default assumption is generally that the business will redeem the shares sold under the plan. However, the available liquidity pool may be supplemented by individual shareholders who are able and willing to purchase additional shares.

- If the business redeems shares, the ownership of all the non-selling shareholders increases on a pro rata basis, resulting in no change to the relative ownership. And, since the business is paying for the shares, the redemption will either reduce the company's liquid assets and/or increase the company's indebtedness. In either case, the redemption changes the financial risk profile of the family business.

- If shares are instead purchased by other family shareholders, the relative ownership of the buying shareholders will increase. Further, the company's financial position is unaffected, since it is serving the role of matchmaker, but is not actually a party to the transaction. If there are shareholders with the financial capacity and willingness to purchase additional shares, the family can benefit from having a liquidity program that does not take capital away from the business.

Frequency

Liquidity may be available on a continuous basis or at specified intervals. A continuous plan provides the most flexibility for shareholders, but restricting redemptions to specific dates (annual or potentially even less frequent) is generally more efficient and predictable for the managers of the business, and allows the business to accumulate capital to fund the redemption.

> Liquidity programs are not cure-alls, but when carefully designed and implemented, they can relieve many of the pressure points that face growing multi-generation family businesses.

Availability

Liquidity plans generally include caps on the aggregate dollar amount of liquidity to be made available, whether to individual shareholders or in total. Higher caps increase the perceived value of the liquidity program to family shareholders, but at the cost of greater uncertainty to the business. As noted above, however, the uncertainty to the business can be hedged, or even eliminated, if some or all of the purchases are made by other shareholders rather than the company.

Terms

Liquidity programs may provide for immediate cash payment, or require the selling shareholder to accept a note upon tendering their shares. While selling shareholders generally prefer cash, using notes (or a combination of notes and cash) increases the company's flexibility and may allow for a larger redemption pool. If the terms of the note issued in exchange for shares feature a below-market interest rate, the economic value of the transaction will be less than the nominal price.

Pricing

Finally, a liquidity program must specify the price at which shares can be sold. There are essentially three options for the price to be paid, and each option has consequences for the selling and non-selling shareholders.

- **Change of Control.** The first option is a change of control value. This is akin to the value in exchange for the business. The change of control value contemplates that potential acquirers may anticipate making changes to the business to increase cash flow. If the acquirer is a so-called strategic acquirer, the magnitude of such changes can be quite large. While selling shareholders would prefer to receive a change of control value, it can be difficult for the company (or purchasing shareholder) to finance the purchase since the business is not actually being sold and will presumably continue to be operated with the existing level of cash flow.

- **As-If Freely Traded.** The second option mimics how the company's shares would be priced if they were traded in the public stock market. If the change of control value is value in exchange, the as-if freely traded value is value in use. The as-if freely traded price contemplates that the business will continue as an independent entity, so incremental benefits to be expected by a potential acquirer are not included in the projected cash flows. While this value is less attractive to selling shareholders, it is more feasible for the purchaser (whether the company or another shareholder) to finance the purchase at this price. If the company is later sold to a strategic acquirer, shareholders taking advantage of the liquidity program may feel taken advantage of themselves.

- **Discounted for Illiquidity.** Finally, the price used in the liquidity program may include a discount to reflect the illiquidity of family business shares. Investors prefer to have the ability to easily sell their shares, so it is widely acknowledged that minority shares in private companies are worth less than otherwise comparable shares that are publicly traded. Redemptions at a discounted price confer an economic benefit upon the non-selling family shareholders. Stated alternatively, use of

Figure 12

Pricing Option	Consequences
Change of Control (*Value in Exchange*)	**Selling Shareholder**: Desirable from perspective of selling shareholders, as it reflects the value they would receive were the company to be sold. **Purchaser**: Since this value incorporates estimated benefits that will not be realized in absence of the company being sold, likely to prove difficult to finance.
As-If Freely Traded (*Value in Use*)	**Selling Shareholder**: Replaces benefits of continued ownership, but eliminates upside potential from sale of the company. Subsequent sale at higher price could contribute to intra-family strife. **Purchaser**: Easier to finance since it reflects benefits from continued operation of the business (i.e., excludes expected benefits accruing to a potential acquirer).
Discounted (*Illiquid Value*)	**Selling Shareholder**: May have a chilling effect on shareholders' willingness to sell as sellers bear the economic cost of illiquidity. **Purchaser**: Purchase at discounted value is accretive to remaining shareholders.

a discounted price imposes an economic penalty on the selling family shareholders. Whether that is desirable or not depends in large part on the family's posture toward selling shareholders (i.e., is selling stock akin to treason?).

Figure 12 summarizes the various consequences of the different pricing options.

There is no inherently "right" choice for the price to be used in a liquidity program. The company's directors should weigh the consequences of the various options noted above against the objectives of the liquidity program for the family.

Implementing the Liquidity Program

An effective and sustainable liquidity program should be predictable. Predictability is achieved by having clearly-defined terms that are well-understood by all interested parties, and having regular appraisals of the company's shares prepared by a qualified independent business valuation expert. A qualified business appraiser will perform periodic valuations on a consistent basis, taking into account the financial performance of the family business, fundamental changes in the operations and outlook for the business and the industry, as well as relevant market changes. At the direction of the company, valuations can be prepared at any (or all) of the three levels noted above.

Implementing a liquidity program increases the importance of shareholder education. If family shareholders are going to have the ability to sell shares, they need to do so on an informed basis. It is essential that selling shareholders have a firm grasp of the company's financial performance and strategy, and understand the key factors that drive the valuation.

Liquidity programs are not cure-alls, but when carefully designed and implemented, they can relieve many of the pressure points that face growing multi-generation family businesses.

Potential Next Steps

- ☐ Identify existing shareholder clienteles and determine the needs, objectives, and preferences of each

- ☐ Assess the company's financial capacity to support an ongoing shareholder liquidity program

- ☐ Determine whether the company or other shareholders will be buyers supporting a shareholder liquidity program

- ☐ Define the frequency, size/availability, and terms of a shareholder liquidity program that best meet the objectives of shareholders and the needs of the business

- ☐ Define the level of value to be used for shareholder liquidity program purchases

- ☐ Obtain a qualified independent business valuation at the selected level of value

- ☐ Design education and communication tools to ensure that shareholders are well-informed regarding the liquidity program

Case Studies

Since 1982, we have been observing and working with successful family companies. Over that period, there aren't many family business scenarios the professionals at Mercer Capital haven't seen. We bring that accumulated experience to bear in our assignments advising family businesses. In the following case studies, we summarize some of our recent engagements.

Using a Shareholder Survey to Help Create Corporate Finance Policy and Promote Family Harmony

Context

We were approached by a long-time client in the following situation. Having been in business for more than 100 years, the Company has a large shareholder base spanning the third through fifth generations and comprising three distinct branches of the family tree. The management team, consisting of both family members and unrelated professional managers, was leading the Company through a multi-year growth strategy that, so far, had been very successful. The strategy was capital intensive, and the Company's financial flexibility was limited as the Company had borrowed significant sums to augment retained earnings in financing the required capital investment. The investments had paid off handsomely, with the value of the Company's shares growing nearly 4x since the trough of the Great Recession. Yet some shareholders, desiring more current income from their illiquid stock in the Company, had grown restless with the persistent reinvestment of earnings to fund further growth.

The Engagement

We worked with management and the board to define a multi-phase engagement to help the Company balance the opportunities available to the business and identify shareholder preferences.

Phase I: Financial Education

The first phase of our engagement was to present an education session for the shareholders at the shareholder annual meeting.

Like many successful multi-generation family businesses, the shareholder base includes some individuals with professional finance experience, but many more educators, engineers, healthcare professionals, and non-profit administrators. In other words, the shareholder base consists of intelligent, well-educated individuals who do not spend their waking hours thinking about financial statements. As a result, the session at the annual meeting was designed to equip those shareholders with a working understanding of key corporate finance topics and a vocabulary with which to express their needs and preferences.

The session explored the inter-relationships among capital structure, capital budgeting, and distribution policy. In the context of the Company's business model, the session focused on the trade-offs inherent in any strategy: risk vs return, and capital appreciation vs yield. In addition to providing a common vocabulary, the education session prepared shareholders for the next phase of our engagement, the confidential shareholder survey.

Phase II: The Shareholder Survey

The second phase of our engagement was to design and administer a confidential shareholder survey. The purpose of the survey was to uncover the needs and preferences of family business shareholders.

Previous surveys that the Company had administered internally were hampered by the family members' natural reticence to speak frankly regarding their perceptions of the Company or their personal cash flow needs. Knowing that individual responses to this survey would not be shared with management, family members were able to share their perceptions and preferences unencumbered by family dynamics.

Importantly, a survey is not the same thing as a shareholder vote—the board was not using the survey to avoid its fiduciary duty to make strategic decisions. Rather, the survey demonstrated the board's desire to solicit preferences to aid in its deliberations.

The survey was divided into four sections. The first collected demographic data on the respondents, and the following sections addressed return expectations, distribution policy, and shareholder liquidity.

Survey Analysis and Reporting

All survey results were submitted directly to Mercer Capital. Our next task was to compile and analyze the results.

In order to preserve confidentiality, we created a presentation that summarized our analysis of the aggregate survey results. Perhaps the most important result of the survey was the discovery of three distinct "clienteles" within the shareholder base that had common economic characteristics with regard to concentrations of income and wealth. These clienteles cut across generational and family lines, revealing unexpected affinities within the shareholder base. Membership in the various clienteles had strong predictive power regarding responses to other survey questions, particularly with respect to preferences for interim distributions and capital appreciation.

Despite the different yield preferences among the different cohorts, the strategic planning committee was reassured by broad consensus throughout the shareholder base along a couple dimensions. First, nearly all family members viewed their shares in the Company differently than other investments. Each family member took pride in being a shareholder.

Second, the shareholders had no appetite for either an outright sale of the Company or diluting the family's collective ownership by soliciting a large equity investment from an institutional investor.

We presented the results of the survey at the annual family retreat. With these survey results in hand, the strategic planning committee was prepared to move to the next phase of the engagement.

Phase III: Peer Benchmarking and Dividend Policy Implementation

Following the survey, we summarized six potential strategic options for the board to consider in light of the observed clientele effect.

As the board deliberated these options, we assisted management in re-visiting the hurdle rate used in their capital budgeting process. We assessed the appropriate hurdle rate by evaluating the implied cost of capital for a group of publicly traded peer companies. We also analyzed the dividend policies of the public peer group to help establish a target dividend yield for the Company.

Of the six potential strategic options we identified, the board opted to slow the pace of capital spending in order to create financial flexibility for the Company and allow for a higher dividend payout ratio. In light of multi-year capital investment commitments, we worked with management to establish a target dividend yield for the Company that appropriately balanced the investment opportunities available to the firm and the desire of shareholders for greater current income.

Outcome for the Shareholders and the Company

At the next annual meeting, we reviewed some of the key financial concepts we had introduced to the shareholders the prior year and summarized the results of our peer benchmarking analysis. In conjunction with management's presentation of financial results for the year and on-going capital investments, we were able to provide much-needed clarity for the shareholders with respect to future distributions.

In summary, our engagement generated a number of benefits for the client:

- A more informed shareholder base understanding the inherent tradeoffs facing the business.

- A structured process for discerning the needs and preferences of the Company's shareholders.

- Identification of three underlying clienteles within the Company's shareholder base, each of which has a common set of economic characteristics, risk tolerances, and distribution preferences.

- A clear articulation of what the Company means to the family shareholders from both economic and non-economic perspectives.

- A more rigorous and disciplined capital budgeting process, including an appropriate market-derived hurdle rate.

- A well-reasoned dividend policy based on relevant peer data, the Company's current financial position, existing capital investment commitments, and the availability of attractive capital investments.

Conclusion

Over the course of the engagement, the Company's shareholders were able to give constructive, frank, and relevant feedback to management and gained a vocabulary for expressing their needs and preferences. As a result, the management and the directors were able to replace the shareholders' uncertainty and growing dissatisfaction regarding dividend policy with a well-defined roadmap for dividends that is transparent and balances the needs and preferences of the diverse shareholder base.

Second Generation Shareholders Achieve Long-Term Sustainability

Context

We received a call from a shareholder in a successful, second generation family business as result of our publications regarding dividend policy. The four second generation owners had purchased the business from their parents a number of years earlier.

The Company was in uncharted territory. The Company had been growing, the acquisition debt was nearly paid off, and the shareholders had differing views regarding the business, the future outlook, and the appropriate dividend policy.

The second generation owners had done some planning of their own, and the CEO, who had led the first-generation buyout and had run the Company for years, was looking forward to transitioning into a board and owner role after bringing on a non-family CEO.

The Engagement

In addition to the four shareholders (each of whom served as directors), the Company had three outside board members with diverse operating and financial experience. So there were two questions for the shareholders and the board, from their differing perspectives.

1. What portion of shareholder returns should come from dividends and what portion from expected capital appreciation?

2. What dividend policy would be reasonable for the Company, given the development of outside management and the need for and opportunities for the Company to grow?

Mercer Capital was retained to help the shareholders and directors address these questions. The engagement was divided into two phases.

Phase I: Financial Discussion and Education

Understanding the Needs of All Stakeholders

First, we met with the shareholders collectively and individually. The purpose was to understand their differing perspectives regarding future dividends from the business. We also spent time talking about the purpose of dividend policy and the various ways in which it could be implemented in a company like theirs.

As the discussions ensued, it became clear that the four shareholders had differing personal perspectives and had followed differing personal investment plans leading to the current point.

One of the shareholders had built a significant, multi-million dollar investment portfolio based on the small, incremental dividends that had been paid over the years that the Company was repaying acquisition debt to the parents. Another of the shareholders had virtually no personal net worth outside the Company, having pursued a different lifestyle philosophy than his siblings. The other two shareholders had modest portfolios outside the business.

There was a disparity in the level of shareholder liquidity outside the Company. We realized that, given the then-current profitability of the business and the retirement of acquisition debt, the Company had substantial free cash flow and substantial value.

We also met with the board of directors, which included the shareholders and the outside members.

Recommendations to Address Shareholder Liquidity Now and in the Future

In the first meeting, we suggested that it might be reasonable to consider a leveraged dividend recapitalization. The purpose of the recapitalization was to provide a substantial, after-tax nest egg of liquidity outside the business for the four shareholders, who owned the business equally.

The discussion then turned to dividend policy on a going forward basis. Since the Company was a tax pass-through entity, the first policy consideration was that the Company should make quarterly distributions to the shareholders to pay for their pass-through tax liabilities. The question then shifted to identifying the appropriate policy for "economic distributions," or dividends in excess of pass-through taxes.

We explained that there were a number of potential policies for consideration. The policies would have to be adjusted to consider the magnitude of the leveraged dividend recapitalization and the prospects for growth. The potential policies included:

1. **Constant dividend payout ratio.** This policy would call for a constant percentage of "net income" (after pass-through taxes) to be paid to shareholders.

2. **Constant dividend yield.** The board could set a target dividend yield (usually based on beginning value) to establish the annual dollar dividend. The yield could be determined based on reference to similar, publicly traded companies or through some other decision-making process.

3. **Annual dollar dividend.** The dividend could be based on board judgment each year. This was not attractive to a couple of the shareholders who did not want to be in annual discussions with management regarding "dividends versus growth."

Upon reviewing our recommendations, the board elected to set a constant dividend yield target. Dividends would rise or fall based on changes in value, which all the shareholders could agree was a reasonable benchmark.

Phase II: Implementation

Given the Company's history of profitable growth, the Company was able to obtain bank financing for a significant (but not reckless) leveraged dividend recapitalization. All debt coverage ratios were easily attainable on a pro forma basis. No shareholder guarantees were required. The financing was straightforward and completed with little difficulty.

The Company established a dividend yield for future economic dividends. The yield was adjusted to account for the debt service on the recapitalization debt and to allow for adequate reinvestment for future growth.

Outcome for the Shareholders and the Company

The engagement accomplished a number of important objectives.

Shareholder Harmony

The shareholders worked together to develop a policy that was reasonable for each of them given their differing personal situations and objectives.

Shareholder Diversification and Liquidity

The leveraged recapitalization enabled each shareholder to set aside a significant nest egg of liquidity independent of his or her ownership of the Company.

Shareholder/Management Harmony

The new, non-family CEO had marching orders from the board regarding expectations for debt service and for shareholder distributions. His "allowance" for capital expenditures was the residual cash flow after debt service and shareholder distributions.

Long-Term Sustainability

The Company and the shareholders had agreement regarding the outlook for the future. With a non-family CEO, this second generation family business had transitioned to a more sustainable footing with four shareholder directors who were not active in management of the business.

Conclusion

We were excited by the opportunity to help this family secure the sustainability of its growing and successful Company. By addressing and listening to the different perspectives of the four shareholders, we were able to promote a balanced financial course of action that addressed each party's concerns and avoid the rancor and distrust that plagues too many family businesses.

Laying a Foundation for the Future

Context

We were engaged by a large family-owned industrial company to assist an internal committee charged with three distinct tasks: (1) develop recommended hurdle rates for capital investment for different operating divisions, (2) develop a recommended capital structure for the business, and (3) assess the existing capital budgeting process and make recommendations for improvements.

Having been in business for more than 50 years, the Company had generated enviable revenue and profit growth under the steady, long-term leadership of its founder. As is often the case, the founder possessed an uncanny intuitive sense for the relevant industry dynamics and the strategic opportunities available to the business. In short, the founder was unique and irreplaceable. While the second generation had made meaningful contributions to the business in recent decades, the second generation members deemed it prudent to transition leadership of the Company to a rising group of professional (non-family) managers, while themselves transitioning to a board oversight role.

As part of this transition process, the Company recognized the need for greater formal structure around many of the financial disciplines that had previously been the product of the founder's personal insights, expertise, and intuition.

The Engagement

The internal committee that we were retained to assist consisted of a group of long-tenured finance and operations managers at the Company. No one on the committee was a member of the founding family, but the committee's recommendations would ultimately be subject to board approval. Directors include members of the second generation and several recently-installed independent directors with deep industry experience.

Over the course of our engagement, we met with the full committee on multiple occasions to present our research findings and solicit input regarding the risk profile, specific concerns, and needs of the Company.

Recommended Hurdle Rates

The committee's first responsibility was to develop recommended hurdle rates for the Company's various operating divisions.

As a first step, we worked with the committee to identify relevant public peer companies for benchmarking. Each major operating division faced a unique set of risks and industry dynamics giving rise to a different set of relevant peer companies.

The committee determined that its hurdle rate recommendations would be rooted in the weighted average cost of capital (WACC) applicable to the various divisions. In order to ensure that the resulting analysis was internally consistent, we elected to begin by calculating the WACC for the overall Company. The WACC is ultimately an opportunity cost, representing the return capital providers would expect from a portfolio of investments with equal risk. As a result, risk analysis took a front seat in our measurement of the WACC.

While beta is a typical measure of risk used in calculating the WACC, the range of observed betas for the public peer companies was wide, reflecting the unique risk attributes of the various companies. As a result, simply relying on a median or average measure for the group would be insufficient. To formalize our risk analysis, we studied the peer companies closely to identify a group of twelve risk factors that were relevant to the overall risk of each company. Using this risk inventory approach, the committee was able to score the client

Company against the peer group relative to each factor, resulting in a richer, more textured risk assessment and beta selection.

Once the consolidated WACC had been measured, the same risk inventory approach was then transposed to the individual operating divisions of the Company. We evaluated each division relative to the consolidated entity with respect to each of the identified risk factors. The result of this analysis was a "top down" view of the WACC for each operating division relative to the consolidated cost of capital. We then supplemented this "top down" view with a "bottom up" approach that focused on the betas, capital structures, and other observable metrics of the division-specific peer groups at a more granular level. The committee selected hurdle rates on the basis of these two complementary perspectives, ensuring that the recommendations reconciled to the consolidated WACC.

Recommended Capital Structure

On a parallel track with the risk assessment and weighted average cost of capital analysis, we developed a recommendation for a target capital structure for the Company. In recent years, the Company had allocated a portion of annual operating cash flows to debt repayment, resulting in a highly-liquid and nearly debt-free balance sheet.

While the lack of financial leverage reduced the Company's overall risk profile, the family and senior managers were concerned that maintaining such a financial posture would dampen future returns as an unwillingness to borrow funds could artificially constrain the amount of capital available to invest in what were deemed to be attractive acquisition opportunities and capital investments. At the same time, the committee was well aware of the costs that come with excessive leverage.

In conjunction with our risk assessment and benchmarking exercise, we analyzed the capital structures of the public peer companies with respect to their operating characteristics, profitability, credit rating, and cost of funding. Balancing these concerns, we helped the committee identify a target capital structure that was prudent, would increase the capital available for investment, and reduce the overall cost of capital for the business.

Capital Budgeting Process Review

The committee's final task was to review the Company's existing capital budgeting process. The Company's legacy project evaluation process reflected in no small measure the unique and irreplaceable perspective and insights of the founder. Through the transition to the next group of managers, the Company deemed it important to enhance the formal structure around the Company's project screening.

We developed and presented recommendations to the committee regarding specific scenarios and areas of concern in project evaluation and screening identified by the committee. Among the topics we addressed were the role of strategy in project evaluation, the use of alternative financial metrics for project evaluation, and identification of relevant project cash flows for analysis.

Conclusion

Our work with the committee was summarized and documented for the board of directors. The board enthusiastically approved the committee's recommendations, which have been implemented throughout the organization. The new hurdle rates, capital structure target, and capital budgeting guidelines are proving to be important elements of the ongoing sustainability of the family business as it transitions to a new era of management oversight and market opportunities.

About the Author

Travis W. Harms, CFA, CPA/ABV, leads Mercer Capital's Family Business Advisory Services Group. Travis's practice focuses on providing financial education, valuation, and other strategic financial consulting to multi-generation family businesses. The Family Business Advisory Services Group helps family shareholder, boards, and management teams align their perspectives on the financial realities, needs, and opportunities of the business.

Travis is also the leader of Mercer Capital's Financial Reporting Valuation Group. His practice here focuses on providing public and private clients with fair value opinions and related assistance pertaining to goodwill and other intangible assets, stock-based compensation, and illiquid financial assets.

Travis is a frequent speaker on valuation and related topics to audiences of business owners, financial executives, auditors, and valuations specialists at professional conferences and other events across the U.S. In addition, Travis performs valuations used for tax compliance, ESOP compliance, and other purposes for clients in a wide range of industries.

Travis is a member of The Appraisal Foundation's working group to address best practices for control premiums, and co-authored the book *Business Valuation: An Integrated Theory*, Second Edition, with Z. Christopher Mercer, FASA, CFA, ABAR.

Family Business Director

Corporate Finance & Planning Insights for
Multi-Generational Family Businesses

Family business directors face a unique set of challenges: the strategic and long-term decisions that fall to any corporate director are overlaid with often complex family dynamics. For public company directors, shareholders are a nameless, faceless group of individuals and institutions "out there," each of whom can come and go at their leisure. By contrast, family business directors bear a fiduciary responsibility to a finite group of siblings, aunts, uncles, cousins, and other kin, with whom they are likely to have some form of ongoing relationship outside of the family business. These very specific shareholders are likely to have very specific preferences and perspectives on the family business. Even non-family, or independent, directors will find that family dynamics intrude upon their decision-making. We suspect the pressures and challenges associated with sitting at the intersection of business and family are under-appreciated.

Owning a successful business can serve as the "glue" that holds a family together across generations and different branches of the family tree. Unfortunately, it can also be a source of contention, strife, and hostility. Within just a couple generations, it is not uncommon for economic interests and preferences among family members to diverge. If family harmony is a good worth pursuing—and we think it is—directors need to acknowledge this diversity of shareholder needs and preferences.

- In our experience, the most consequential decisions that family business directors make relate to dividend policy. But dividend policy for family businesses is never just about dividends. Dividend policy touches on the core of what the family business "means" to the family. Does your family business exist to grow, keeping up with the growth of your family as generations multiply through time? Or, does your family business exist to provide financial independence to current family members through substantial dividends?

- Dividend policy decisions are not made in a vacuum. If the quarterly dividend check is the picture that gets shareholder attention, corporate reinvestment is the negative image of that picture. Cash that is paid to family shareholders as dividends cannot be reinvested to grow the business, while cash reinvested in the business for future growth cannot be distributed to family shareholders. So, every decision about dividend policy is also a decision about corporate reinvestment. We refer to this as capital allocation.

- Capital structure is the release value when there are tensions between dividend policy and capital allocation. Family business directors are responsible for deciding how to finance the portfolio of assets that is the family business.

Dividend policy, capital allocation, and capital structure are so inter-related that disagreement about any of them is really disagreement about all of them. Every post we write will aim to help family business directors think about these fundamental corporate finance decisions in a fresh light, and apply these insights to their unique circumstances to enhance the sustainability of their family business and preserve family harmony.

Learn More & Subscribe for Weekly Updates
mer.cr/fbdirector

Mercer Capital's
Family Business
Advisory Services

Mercer Capital provides sophisticated corporate finance services to family businesses.

We have had the privilege of working with successful family and closely held businesses for over 35 years. We help family business directors make better dividend policy, capital allocation, and capital structure decisions that are tailored to the unique circumstances and needs of your family and business.

Services

Customized Board Advisory Services

We help you and your fellow directors understand the implications of the decisions you are called upon to make. We work with you to frame the decision to promote better outcomes, and help you formulate the relevant questions that need to be addressed and answered during board deliberations concerning your dividend policy, capital allocation, and capital structure decisions.

Management Consulting

We work with family business management teams to assess hurdle rates, develop sustainable capital budgeting processes, and evaluate potential acquisitions & divestitures.

Independent Valuation Opinions

We provide independent, unbiased, and reliable valuation opinions for gift & estate tax planning, buy-sell agreements, and shareholder liquidity programs.

Transaction Advisory Services

When an attractive offer arises, we work with family business directors to respond to acquisition offers, evaluate strategic alternatives, provide fairness and solvency opinions, and manage the marketing and sale of family businesses.

Confidential Shareholder Surveys

By designing, administering, and summarizing the results of a confidential shareholder survey, we solicit relevant and timely shareholder feedback so you and your fellow directors can make fully-informed decisions in light of the preferences and risk tolerances of your family shareholders.

Benchmarking / Business Intelligence

We turn available financial data from publicly traded peers and other sources into relevant information that helps you and your fellow directors make better corporate finance decisions.

Shareholder Engagement

If your family business is to function as a source of unity rather than division, your family shareholders need to be positively engaged with the business. We develop and provide customized financial education for your family shareholders. We present at family council meetings, shareholder meetings, and other gatherings on a wide variety of topics ranging from how to read your company's financial statements to primers on the weighted average cost of capital, return on invested capital, and other topics.

Shareholder Communication Support

Poor communication is the most common cause of family shareholder angst. We help family business directors identify the appropriate frequency, format and content of financial reporting to shareholders. Making financial results accessible, understandable, and relevant to family shareholders is essential to achieving and preserving family harmony.

Contact a Mercer Capital professional to discuss your needs in confidence.

Mercer Capital's Family Business Advisory Team

Travis W. Harms, CFA, CPA/ABV
(901) 322-9760
harmst@mercercapital.com

Timothy R. Lee, ASA
(901) 322-9740
leet@mercercapital.com

Z. Christopher Mercer, FASA, CFA, ABAR
(901) 685-2120
mercerc@mercercapital.com

Nicholas J. Heinz, ASA
(901) 685-2120
heinzn@mercercapital.com

CPSIA information can be obtained
at www.ICGtesting.com
Printed in the USA
LVHW081214110319
610201LV00004B/4/P